lonel

P

BARCELONA

TOP EXPERIENCES • LOCAL LIFE

ISABELLA NOBLE

Contents

Plan Your Trip 4

Palau de la Música Catalana (p84)
ISABEL TALLEDA GUERRERO/GETTY IMAGES ©

Welcome to Barcelona

Barcelona is a whirlwind of dream-like Modernista architecture, sun-toasted beaches and lamplit medieval streets hiding irresistible restaurants, bars, boutiques and more. The endlessly captivating Catalan capital holds ancient Roman ruins, modern-architecture masterpieces, Gothic palaces, entrancing galleries and one of the world's most venerated football stadiums – yet still it dazzles with neighbourhood markets, gorgeous green spaces and village-vibe squares.

Carrer del Bisbe (p45)

Barcelona's Top Experiences

Marvel at Gaudí's spectacular Sagrada Família (p110)

Dive into the Museu Picasso's art and architecture (p74)

Be dazzled by Gaudí's La Pedrera (p114)

Soak up the scene on El Poblenou's beaches (p94)

Get lost in the beauty of Casa Batlló (p116)

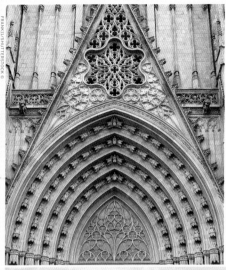

Marvel at the magnificent Catedral de Barcelona (p42)

Explore magical Park Güell (p134)

Uncover masterpieces at the Museu Nacional d'Art de Catalunya (p160)

BRIAN KINNEY/SHUTTERSTOCK ©

STEVE LOVEGROVE/SHUTTERSTOCK ©

Savour history at the Basílica de Santa Maria del Mar (p78)

Wander into Miró's imagination at the Fundació Joan Miró (p162)

Dig into La Rambla's history (p40)

Dining Out

PAULZHUK/SHUTTERSTOCK ©

Barcelona's food scene is fuelled by leading chefs, superb markets and magnificent ingredients. Catalan culinary masterminds, such as Ferran and Albert Adrià, and Carles Abellán, are icons, while classic Catalan recipes and creative international flavours also earn accolades. The city's food world continues to thrive, thrill and innovate.

New Catalan Cuisine

Avant-garde chefs have made Catalonia famous across the world for their food laboratories. Here the notion of gourmet cuisine is deconstructed, as chefs transform liquids and solid foods into foams, create an 'ice cream' of classic ingredients by means of liquid nitrogen and employ spherification to create unusual and artful morsels. This alchemical cookery is known as molecular gastronomy.

Classic Catalan Cuisine

Traditional Catalan recipes showcase the great produce of the Mediterranean without any fuss: fish, prawns, cuttlefish, clams, pork, game, olive oil, peppers, tomatoes and garlic. Classic dishes also feature unusual pairings (seafood with meat, fruit with fowl).

Tapas

Tapas (pictured above), those bite-sized morsels of joy, are not a typical Catalan concept, but tapas bars nonetheless abound across Barcelona. *Platillos* (sharing plates) are also popular, often overlapping with tapas, while many wine and vermouth bars double as tapas bars. Wonderful *pintxo* (Basque tapas) bars are dotted around too, particularly along Poble Sec's Carrer de Blai.

Best Catalan

Can Recasens Superb local cooking, romantic Poblenou setting. (p102)

La Pubilla Lightly creative classics in Gràcia. (p140)

Cinc Sentits Jordi Artal's Michelin-star cuisine

highlights Catalan produce. (p125)

Bar Muy Buenas Catalan faves amid 1920s decor. (p61)

Elisabets Traditional Catalan classics. (p61)

Suculent Superb, modern Catalan cuisine. (p65)

Informal Creative Catalan cuisine from a prize-winning chef. (p51)

Best Tapas

Quimet i Quimet Mouth-watering morsels for a standing crowd. (p170)

Gresca Creative bites, natural wines, bistro vibe. (p125)

Tapas 24 Everyone's favourite gourmet tapas bar. (p126)

Pepa Natural wines meet ambitious bites in L'Eixample. (p125)

Bar del Pla A touch of creativity in La Ribera. (p81)

Cañete Contemporary twists in El Raval. (p65)

Denassus Elegant tapas and organic wines in Poble Sec. (p172)

Extra Bar Creative plates in Gràcia. (p140)

La Cova Fumada An unmissable Barceloneta classic. (p97)

Mercat de la Boqueria For legendary El Quim and Bar Pinotxo. (p49)

Casa de Tapas Cañota Seafood sensations, Galician wines. (p171)

Bar Mut Season-inspired tapas in north L'Eixample. (p127)

Betlem Dreta de L'Eixample favourite. (p127)

Best Gastronomy

Disfrutar Catalan cuisine at its most experimental. (p124)

Lasarte The ultimate fine-dining experience. (p124)

Enigma Travel through Albert Adrià's culinary imagination. (p169)

Mont Bar Homegrown ingredients become exquisite cooking. (p125)

Cocina Hermanos Torres Culinary wizardry in Les Corts. (pictured above; p156)

Alkímia An innovative spin on classics, by Jordi Vilà. (p171)

Bar Open

MICHAEL HEFFERNAN/LONELY PLANET ©

Fun-loving Barcelona is a city for nightlife lovers, with an enticing spread of candlelit wine bars, old-school vermouth taverns, magical cocktail hangouts, stylish roof-terrace lounges and kaleidoscopic clubs where patrons party till daybreak. For something more sedate, teahouses and speciality coffee spots make a fine retreat.

Bars & Lounges

Barcelona has a dizzying assortment of bars. Where to go depends as much on the crowd as it does on the ambience – and whether you want to drink at the latest hot spot (try Sant Antoni), dive into Barcelona's bohemian scene (El Raval) or hang out with the international crowd (Gràcia and El Born). Sometimes, it's a matter of grabbing any empty table on a pretty square.

Cocktail, Wine & Cava Bars

Barcelona's crafted-cocktail scene has exploded in recent years, with prize-winning cocktail bars working their magic in El Born, Gràcia, El Raval and L'Eixample. Wine bars scattered around the city showcase the finest grapes from Spain and beyond. Bars serving mostly natural, organic and/or biodynamic wines are surging in popularity. *Cava* bars tend to be more about the festive ambience than the actual drinking of *cava,* a sparkling white or rosé. And don't forget the vermouth bars (p17).

Clubs

Barcelona's *discotecas* (clubs) are at their best from Thursday to Saturday. Well-known clubs are spread across L'Eixample, Zona Alta and the old city's labyrinth; many bars also morph into dance spots as the night goes on. At the Port Olímpic, a strip of noisy waterfront clubs (Pacha, Opium, CDLC, Catwalk, Shôko) attract raucous crowds, but these venues may be closing down.

MAKSLOGVINOV/SHUTTERSTOCK ©

Best Wine

Perikete Lively wine and tapas bar in Barceloneta. (p105)

Viblioteca A trendy Gràcia space for wine and cheese. (p146)

Bar Zim Pint-sized, cave-like Barri Gòtic wine bar. (p54)

Can Paixano House rosé (and perfect tapas) in La Barceloneta. (p97)

El Diset A wonderland of Catalan wines. (p90)

El Xampanyet Cram in for *cava* and tapas. (pictured above left; p81)

Bar Salvatge Wines on Gràcia's Carrer de Verdi. (p146)

Best Cocktails

Paradiso Walk through a fridge to this glam speak-easy. (p88)

Two Schmucks Pop-up cocktail bar turned Raval sensation. (p68)

Sips Cutting-edge cocktails in a get-involved setting. (p128)

Dr Stravinsky The place to linger over an avant-garde concoction. (p89)

Bar Boadas An iconic drinking den since the 1930s. (p54)

14 de la Rosa Graceful Gràcia fave; also does vermouth, Catalan wines and tapas. (p145)

Best Dancing

La Terrrazza Party beneath palms in the Poble Espanyol. (p174)

Arena Two side-by-side LGBTIQ+ faves in the 'Gaixample'. (p29)

Sala Apolo Gorgeous dance hall with electro, funk and more. (p175)

Moog Small Raval club that draws a dance-loving crowd. (p69)

Marula Café Funk and soul in the Gòtic. (p54)

Best Coffee

Nømad Cøffee Lab & Shop Barcelona's speciality coffee king. (p89)

SlowMov Sustainable, original Gràcia roaster. (p144)

Satan's Coffee Corner In Barri Gòtic and L'Eixample. (p53)

Dalston Coffee Takeaway hit in El Raval. (p68)

Three Marks Loved for its Barcelona-roasted beans. (p128)

Barcelona in a Glass: Vermouth

Based on red or white wine, vermouth is infused with botanicals and fortified with brandy.

The perfect vermouth is usually served over ice, with an olive and a slice of orange.

Vermouth is always accompanied by light snacks, such as tapas of croquettes, anchovies, *patates braves* (potatoes in a spicy tomato sauce) or salty crisps.

La hora del vermut (the hour of vermouth) is as much about the intimate social scene and who you're drinking with as the drink itself.

Vermouth in Spain tends to come from fairly small, local producers; many bars even make their own.

★ Best Places to Drink Vermouth

Quimet i Quimet (p170) Vermouth pairs with montaditos in Poble Sec.

Gràcia (p144) Some of the best bars.

Bar Calders (p173) Lively Sant Antoni hub with perfect vermouth.

Bodega La Peninsular (p103) Fave for vermouth and tapas in Barceloneta.

Morro Fi (p157) Local *vermuteria* with its own label and four branches.

Bormouth (p81) El Born haunt pairing its own vermouth with tasty tapas.

La Mari Ollero (p74) Vermouth with an Andalucian twist on Paral·lel.

Salut!

Arriving from Italy in the mid-19th century, vermouth became a favourite of Barcelona's working class in the years prior to the Spanish Civil War. Though it then fell out of favour, the drink has experienced a revival over the last decade. Now, new vermouth bars are opening all over town; historical vermouth joints are more popular than ever; and artisan varieties are on the up. Join the *barcelonins* to *fer el vermut* (make the vermouth), a sociable event that occurs around noon.

Vermouth and appetisers

JOSE MONTORO/SHUTTERSTOCK ©

CLAUDIOVALDES/SHUTTERSTOCK ©

Treasure Hunt

Barcelona's creative side is on show with its vibrant, understated shopping scene. The Ciutat Vella, L'Eixample and Gràcia host independent boutiques, historic shops, original stores, gourmet corners, designer labels and more. A raft of young creatives have set up boutiques and workshops in El Raval, El Born, Sant Antoni and Gràcia.

Vintage Fashion

El Raval is Barcelona's vintage fashion epicentre, where irresistible old-time stores mingle with a colourful array of affordable, mostly secondhand fashion boutiques, particularly along Carrer de la Riera Baixa and Carrer dels Tallers. The Barri Gòtic is a growing vintage-fashion haven, and you'll also find vintage specialists in El Born (pictured), Gràcia and Sant Antoni.

Markets

Barcelona's 39 fresh-produce markets count among Europe's best. Every neighbourhood has its own central market, which doubles as a local meeting point, and the architecture is often as much an attraction as the tasty things for sale. Look beyond La Rambla's famous Mercat de la Boqueria to find jewels in other districts – a guided food tour is a great way to dive into them.

Boutique Barcelona

The heart of the Barri Gòtic has always been busy with small-scale merchants, these days joined by a raft of international chains. Some of the most curious old shops, such as purveyors of hats, shoes and candles, lurk in the narrow lanes around Plaça de Sant Jaume, while antiques shops line Carrer de la Palla and Carrer dels Banys Nous. La Ribera is home to a cornucopia of old-style specialist food and drink shops, as well as stylish fashion and homewares boutiques, many with a sustainable ethos that champions local artisans and designers. Gràcia

OLEIVA/ALAMY STOCK PHOTO ©

has a similarly local-oriented independent shopping scene with an eco focus.

Best Fashion & Homewares

La Manual Alpargatera Shop the Barri Gòtic for *espardenyes* (espadrilles). (p55)

Ozz Barcelona One of El Born's slow-fashion faves. (p90)

TheAvant Chic women's designer wear. (p130)

Olokuti A Gràcia pioneer in fairtrade pieces. (p147)

Grey Street Carefully curated homewares in El Raval. (p70)

Le Swing One of the Gòtic's vintage stars. (p56)

Bagués-Masriera Exquisite jewellery with a long tradition. (p122)

Best Markets

Mercat de Santa Caterina La Ribera's colourful alternative to La Boqueria. (p84)

Mercat de Sant Antoni Beautifully restored neighbourhood market. (p168)

Mercat de la Llibertat Gràcia's 19th-century beauty, with tapas bars. (p139)

Mercat de la Concepció Known for its lovely out-the-front flower stalls. (p122)

Mercat de Galvany A little-visited 1927 Sant Gervasi delight. (p154)

Mercat dels Encants Sprawling Poblenou flea market. (p107)

Mercat de la Barceloneta Buzzy local food market near the beach. (p97)

Best Food & Wine

Casa Gispert Roast nuts, chocolate, conserves, olive oils and more. (p91)

Vila Viniteca El Born's cathedral of Spanish wines. (p91)

Casa Carot Superb small-producer cheeses and other Catalan delights. (p57)

El Magnífico Barcelona's original coffee roastery, in El Born. (p91)

Escribà Pastries, cakes and Modernisme. (p41)

Fromagerie Can Luc World-roaming cheeses in Gràcia. (p147)

For Kids

Barcelona's Mediterranean attitude means kids are welcome and often join in at restaurants and festivals. Babies and toddlers will be showered with attention. It's a great city for older kids and teens too, who can join for many activities, such as eating late meals. Adjust your children to Barcelona time; otherwise they'll miss half of what's worth seeing.

SYLVAIN SONNET/GETTY IMAGES ©

Dining Out with Kids

Barcelona – and Spain in general – is super friendly when it comes to eating with children. Locals take their kids out all the time and don't worry too much about keeping them up late. Spanish kids tend to eat the Mediterranean offerings enjoyed by their parents, but many restaurants have children's menus that serve up burgers, pizzas, chips, tomato-sauce pasta and the like; some places even have a kids' *menú del dia*. Good local – and childproof – options are *truita de patates/tortilla de patatas* (potato omelette), *pa amb tomàquet/pan con tomate* (bread rubbed with tomato and olive oil) and *croquetes/croquetas* (croquettes).

Practical Matters

○ Nappies (diapers), dummies, creams and formula can be bought at any of the city's many pharmacies and supermarkets (the latter are often a bit cheaper).

○ Barcelona's metro is accessible and great for families with pushchairs. Be mindful of pickpockets.

○ The narrow streets of the Ciutat Vella, with their unpredictable traffic and cobbled streets, are less pushchair-friendly than the rest of Barcelona.

○ Some restaurants and other venues have baby-changing tables, but certainly not all. Most places can rustle up a high chair.

○ Many Spanish women breastfeed in public.

ISTOCK/GETTY IMAGES PLUS ©

Best Attractions

Beaches Plenty of sand and gentle waters. (p26)

La Sagrada Família Gaudí's castle-like cathedral. (p110)

CosmoCaixa A fantastic science museum in the Zona Alta. (p153)

Poble Espanyol Travel through a mini Spain. (p168)

Museu Picasso Older kids will love this outstanding museum in El Born. (p74)

Parc d'Atraccions Tibidabo A fabulous funfair with views. (p153)

Best Parks & Open Spaces

Parc de la Ciutadella Super-central park with a playground, lake, zoo and more. (p84)

Park Güell Glittering colours and *Hansel and Gretel*–like gatehouses. (pictured top left; p134)

Montjuïc Gardens, viewpoints and the fantastical Castell de Montjuïc. (p168)

Gràcia The many village-like squares are great for cavorting kids. (p136)

Font Màgica This light show is guaranteed to make little ones shout 'Again!' (p168)

Parc Natural de Collserola A mountainous pine-sprinkled park in the north. (p153)

Parc del Turó Local-feel park with a lily pond and lovely cafe. (p154)

Parc del Laberint d'Horta Park with its own cypress-edged labyrinth. (p143)

Best Ways to See the City

By Bike Barcelona has tonnes of bike tours and hire outlets. (p28)

By Cable Car Travel up Montjuïc from Barceloneta beach through the air. (pictured top right; p181)

Cuca de Llum High-tech lightworm-like funicular to whisk you up Tibidabo. (p153)

Festes de la Mercè Barcelona's September festival has dancing giants, fire-spitting *correfocs*, kids' workshops and more. (p67)

Responsible Travel

LITTLEAOM/SHUTTERSTOCK ©

In 2019, Barcelona received 12 million tourists, in a city with a population of only 1.62 million. Tourism remains a key part of the local economy, but overtourism has reached a crisis point, particularly in the Ciutat Vella. The city is working towards a more sustainable model that prioritises local residents and finds a much-needed balance.

Combating Overtourism

Barcelona is a year-round city. By exploring outside the peak months (May to September and Easter), you'll find fewer crowds and help spread tourism across the year. October is lovely, and winter is full of festive fun.

Find responsible accommodation, as tourist apartments and illegal lets are driving up rents for locals. Staying in a hotel or family-owned guesthouse supports local workers and businesses. If you'd still prefer to rent, check whether your accommodation is officially registered first (www.fairtourism. barcelona). (p179)

The rest of Catalonia is beautiful and endlessly varied. Stay on to visit soulful Girona, Roman Tarragona, the spectacular Pyrenees, the little-touristed Ebro Delta region, and more.

Use pre-trip research to read up on Barcelona's ongoing sustainable tourism projects and responsible travel tips (https://meet. barcelona.cat).

Support Local & Give Back

Barcelona has many volunteering projects that visitors can get involved in (www.barcelona.cat/en/ getinvolved), including beach clean-ups, such as Clean Beach Initiative (https:// cleanbeachinitiative.org).

Do your research before jumping in.

Enjoy a guided tour (p28) and support local experts at the same time – from historians to architects to chefs.

Rising rents have closed down some of Barcelona's best-known traditional shops. Shop at long-established favourites with special preservation status (p57).

Barcelona's dining scene is a local-produce feast. At most independent restaurants, ingredients come straight from local markets and fish docks. Keep an eye out for restaurants that follow the Slow Food ethos (https://slowfood. barcelona).

Support integration programmes through dining out. Run by not-for-profit organisation Mescladís, **Espai Mescladís** is a lovely Mediterranean cafe that revolves around hospitality-training programmes for those struggling to access the job market (including undocumented migrants). (p88)

Neighbourhood markets show off Barcelona's great pantry. Stock up on local goodies for the kitchen, and find preloved fashion and homewares at markets like El Raval's **El Flea** (p71) and Poblenou's **Mercat dels Encants** (p107). Each weekend, local artists sell their works at the **Mostra d'Art Pintors del Pi**, where there's also a bimonthly Km0 (a term referring to locally produced food that has not travelled far) **food market**. (p56)

Learn More

Around 20% of Spain's homeless population lives in Barcelona. Hidden City Tours trains guides who have been part of the city's homeless community; sensitive tours of the Barri Gòtic and El Raval are interwoven with the guides' own stories, showing a side of Barcelona unseen by most visitors (www. hiddencitytours.com).

Uncover local Roma culture. El Raval's EMUGBA (EcoMuseu Urbà Gitano de Barcelona; www. museuvirtualgitano.cat) celebrates the history and heritage of the city's Roma community with photographs, films, letters and other displays.

Getting Around

Leaving a light footprint is easy in Barcelona. While the city's bike-share scheme Bicing isn't aimed at tourists, there are plenty of local bike-hire operators such as **Bike Tours Barcelona** (www.biketoursbarcelona. com). Public transport is excellent, with metro lines and buses taking you everywhere.

Climate Change & Travel

It's impossible to ignore the impact we have when travelling, and the importance of making changes where we can.

Lonely Planet urges all travellers to engage with their travel carbon footprint. There are many carbon calculators online that allow travellers to estimate the carbon emissions generated by their journey; try resurgence.org/resources/carbon-calculator.html. Many airlines and booking sites offer travellers the option of offsetting the impact of greenhouse gas emissions by contributing to climate-friendly initiatives around the world.

We continue to offset the carbon footprint of all Lonely Planet staff travel, while recognising this is a mitigation more than a solution.

Architecture

VALERYEGOROV/GETTY IMAGES ©

Barcelona is dotted with striking Gothic cathedrals, fantastical Modernista creations and avant-garde buildings. Building first boomed in the late Middle Ages. In the late 19th century whimsical Modernisme arrived. The third notable era began in the late 1980s and continues today. Dive in on an expert-led guided tour (p28).

Best Gothic

Catedral de Barcelona The old city's Gothic centrepiece, at once extravagant and sombre. (p42)

Basílica de Santa Maria del Mar Arguably the high point of Catalan Gothic. (p78)

Basílica de Santa Maria del Pi A 14th-century jewel with a dazzling rose window. (p45)

Museu Marítim In the former Gothic shipyards just off La Rambla. (p100)

Reial Monestir de Santa Maria de Pedralbes A 14th-century monastery with a superb three-level cloister. (p153)

Museu Picasso Rare Gothic mansions, now converted. (p74)

Best of Gaudí

La Sagrada Família Gaudí's unfinished symphony. (p110)

La Pedrera Showpiece Gaudí building with an otherworldly roof. (p114)

Casa Batlló Eye-catching facade with an astonishing interior. (p116)

Casa Vicens Gaudí's original, Unesco-listed commission. (pictured; p139)

Park Güell The great architect's playfulness in full swing. (p134)

Palau Güell Gaudí's only building in the old part of town. (p63)

Bellesguard Less-visited, castle-like jewel in the Zona Alta. (p153)

Best of the Modernista Rest

Palau de la Música Catalana Breathtaking concert hall by Lluís Domènech i Montaner. (p84)

Casa Amatller Josep Puig i Cadafalch's neighbour to Casa Batlló (p122)

Casa Lleó Morera Domènech i Montaner's dancing nymphs, cupolas and stained glass. (p122)

Fundació Antoni Tàpies Brick and iron-framed masterpiece by Domènech i Montaner. (p122)

Recinte Modernista de Sant Pau Gilded pavilions by Domènech i Montaner. (p122)

Museums & Galleries

Thanks to its rich heritage, Barcelona boasts an array of world-class museums and galleries, from journeys into Catalan history to an exploration of some of Spain's great creative minds, including Pablo Picasso, Joan Mirò, Salvador Dalí and Antoni Tàpies. The line between museum and gallery is blurred, and the buildings themselves are highlights.

TOMASSEREDA/GETTY IMAGES ©

Best Art & Design

Museu Picasso A journey through Picasso's early work. (p74)

Fundació Joan Miró From formative years to later works. (p162)

Fundació Antoni Tàpies A selection of bold works. (p122)

Museu Nacional d'Art de Catalunya Modern Catalan art at Barcelona's premier gallery. (pictured; p160)

MACBA Fabulous contemporary collection; El Raval's street art. (p63)

Museu Can Framis Catalan artists in a reimagined 18th-century factory. (p101)

Moco Museum Modern and street art; 16th-century palace. (p85)

CCCB Excellent rotating exhibitions, often photography. (p64)

CaixaForum Dynamic artistic space in a converted Modernista building. (p168)

Best History Museums

Museu d'Història de Barcelona Roman ruins and Gothic architecture. (p48)

Museu Marítim In the Gothic former shipyards. (p100)

Museu d'Història de Catalunya Wonderful ode to Catalan history. (p100)

MUHBA Refugi 307 Barcelona's best-preserved air-raid shelter. (p169)

Museu d'Arqueologia de Catalunya Curious finds from across Catalonia. (p168)

Camp Nou Unravel the history of FC Barcelona. (p155)

Top Tip: Articket BCN

Barcelona's best bargain for art lovers is the **Articket BCN** (www.articketbcn.org; €35), which covers six major galleries.

Parks & Beaches

Once you move beyond the Ciutat Vella's tight tangle of streets, Barcelona opens up as a city awash with light. Its parks, gardens and golden beaches lend it a Mediterranean air and make popular escapes. Meanwhile, the ongoing Superilles (Superblocks) project is creating a network of green spaces that prioritise pedestrians all over the city.

ISTOCK EDITORIAL/GETTY IMAGES PLUS ©

Best Parks & Gardens

Park Güell Zany Gaudí flourishes meet landscape gardening. (p134)

Parc de la Ciutadella Home to parliament, a zoo and public art. (p84)

Parc Natural de Collserola Protected wild space for hiking and biking. (p153)

Jardins de Mossèn Cinto de Verdaguer Gentle, sloping Montjuïc flower gardens. (p165)

Jardins de Laribal Alhambra-inspired gardens halfway up Montjuïc. (p165)

Parc del Laberint d'Horta An 18th-century delight with a maze. (p143)

Parc del Turó Water lilies beneath soaring trees in Sant Gervasi. (p154)

Best Beaches

El Poblenou Platges Lovely golden beaches stretching northeast from the centre. (p94)

Platja de la Barceloneta Arrive early to savour this sunny old-timer without crowds. (pictured, with W Hotel – architect: Ricardo Bofill; p97)

Zona de Banys El Fòrum's twinkling seawater swimming area. (p95)

Beaches Beyond Barcelona

Many of the area's beaches lie outside the centre. Visit on a day trip, taking *rodalies* (trains) R1 or R2 from Plaça de Catalunya and Passeig de Gràcia respectively.

Platja de Castelldefels Around 20km southwest of central Barcelona; loved by kitesurfers.

Sitges Spain's most famous LGBTIQ+ beach town, 35km southwest of Barcelona.

Platja del Garraf Tiny Garraf village, 30km southwest of Barcelona, trickles down to a sparkling teal bay bordered by striking green-and-white 1920s beach huts.

Montgat Around 20km northeast of Barcelona, on the Costa del Maresme.

Under the Radar Barcelona

Once visitor numbers return to pre-pandemic levels, overtourism will once again be a concern for Barcelona. By exploring beyond heavily touristed areas (particularly the Ciutat Vella), you'll help build more responsible tourism and a sustainable local environment while uncovering seldom-visited neighbourhood restaurants and architectural jewels.

JOAN_BAUTISTA/SHUTTERSTOCK ©

Outer Neighbourhoods

Staying in less touristed *barris* in outer Barcelona gives you the chance to tap into local life, support small neighbourhood businesses, explore quieter sights and gain a broader perspective of the city. Smart Sarrià-Sant Gervasi in northwest Barcelona, peaceful northern Horta, low-key Poblenou and the Sants/Les Corts area west of the centre make excellent bases, as does sprawling L'Eixample. There are even worthwhile hotels on Tibidabo's slopes.

Fun Alternatives

Parc Natural de Collserola Hike and bike the vast green expanses. (p153)

Beaches Head to sands further out of town.

Pedralbes Explore a 14th-century convent (pictured) and lesser-known Gaudí sights. (p153)

El Poblenou Check out the creative scene and neighbourhood restaurants. (p93)

Poble Sec Tap into the buzzy dining scene and sloping streets. (p159)

Sants Modernista market, excellent restaurants and bars, and an elevated *rambla*. (p174)

Sarrià-Sant Gervasi Well-heeled former villages, Gaudí's Bellesguard and more. (p157)

Parc del Laberint d'Horta Visit the garden labyrinth, and the farmhouse restaurants of Horta. (p143)

Bangkok Cafe Try Barcelona's top Thai restaurant and explore the main square and market in Les Corts. (p156)

Tours & Courses

A wonderful way to get to know Barcelona (and support small-scale initiatives and businesses) is to join a guided tour led by a local expert. Options cover all kinds of interests, from Barcelona gastronomy and local history to street art and the city's design world. The wealth of specialised local courses is another way to peel back the city's layers.

DAVID J. LEW/500PX ©

Tours

Devour (https://devourtours.com) Neighbourhood-focused food tours.

Barcelona Architecture Walks (https://barcelonarchitecturewalks.com) Design-led itineraries.

Culinary Backstreets (https://culinarybackstreets.com) Outstanding food walks.

Hidden City Tours (www.hiddencitytours.com) Guides who have been part of Barcelona's homeless community.

Runner Bean Tours (www.runnerbeantours.com; by donation; [🚶]) Thematic pay-what-you-wish tours.

Barcelona Design Tours (www.barcelonadesigntours.com) Uncover the city's creative side.

Street Art in El Raval Walking routes and workshops led by artists (p64).

Civil War Tours (http://thespanishcivilwar.com) Learn about this dark period with expert Nick Lloyd.

Cap A Mar (https://capamarbcn.com) Great tours showcasing Barceloneta's maritime heritage.

Bike Tours Barcelona (www.biketoursbarcelona.com) A cycling-tour original.

Molokai SUP Center (www.molokaisupcenter.com) Join kayaking outings.

Orsom (www.barcelona-orsom.com) Year-round catamaran trips.

Uncensored Barcelona (https://uncensoredtours.net) Insightful Ciutat Vella (pictured; Pont del Bisbe) tours using recycled bikes.

Courses & Classes

Barcelona Cooking (www.barcelonacooking.net; [🚶]) Cooking classes run by three Galician friends.

Alblanc Atelier (www.alblancatelier.com) and **Passage Flowers** (https://passageflowers.com) offer flower workshops.

Working in the Redwoods (www.workingintheredwoods.com) Ceramicist Miriam Cernuda runs occasional classes.

Casa Protea (www.casaprotea.com) Creative workshops in Gràcia.

Paella Club (https://thepaellaclub.com) Master the art of paella-making with a hands-on class in El Raval.

LGBTIQ+ Barcelona

Barcelona has a vibrant LGBTIQ+ scene, with an array of bars, clubs, restaurants and bookshops in the 'Gaixample', an area of L'Eixample around Carrer del Consell de Cent. Other LGBTIQ+ venues are dotted around Sant Antoni, Poble Sec and beyond, while Platja de la Mar Bella (p95) is the community's go-to beach.

CARLOS PEREIRA M/SHUTTERSTOCK ©

Best Bars

La Monroe (p69) Stylish, low-key, all-welcoming bar in El Raval's Filmoteca.

La Chapelle (Map p120, C6) Casual Gaixample spot for cocktails.

La Federica (www. facebook.com/ barlafederica) A Poble Sec favourite of the local LGBTIQ+ scene; tapas, cocktails and performances.

Punto BCN (Map p120, C6; www.grupoarena.com) Good mix of ages and creeds in the Gaixample.

Candy Darling (Map p120, D6; www.facebook.com/ candydarlingbar) Culture-focused indie LGBTIQ+ bar with drag shows and music performances.

Carita Bonita (Map p120, D4) Popular, weekend-only lesbian bar for drinks and dancing.

Best Parties

Arena Madre (Map p120, E5; www.grupoarena.com) Drag shows, dancing and more at this top LGBTIQ+ club.

Arena Classic (Map p120, E5; www.grupoarena.com) Buzzing LGBTIQ+ club hosting plenty of lesbian events.

Pride Barcelona (www. pridebarcelona.org) Two weeks of summer celebrations (pictured).

Circuit (https:// circuitfestival.net) Hugely popular August festival.

Top Tip: LGBTIQ+ Sitges

Spain's LGBTIQ+ capital is saucily hedonistic Sitges, 35km southwest of Barcelona and linked by frequent trains (45 minutes). This attractive town is on the international party circuit and hosts some fabulous LGBTIQ+-oriented beaches, a raucous Carnaval in February/March, and its own Pride march in June.

Four Perfect Days

Day 1

Day 2

Hit the Barri Gòtic early. Explore the **Cathedral** (p42), **El Call** (p50) and **Museu d'Història de Barcelona** (p48). **La Rambla** (p40) and the **Mercat de la Boqueria** (pictured; p49) are also quietest first thing. Lunch at **Brugarol** (p50), **Bar Celta** (p52) or **La Plata** (p51).

Wander over to El Born, where treasures include the **Basílica de Santa Maria del Mar** (p78), **Museu Picasso** (p74) and **Moco Museum** (p85).

Don't miss the **Mercat de Santa Caterina** (p84), or tapas at **Bar del Pla** (p81) and **El Xampanyet** (p81). End at **Bar Sauvage** (p89) or **Paradiso** (p88), or catch a concert at the **Palau de la Música Catalana** (p84).

Start with Gaudí's **La Sagrada Família** (p110), ideally on a guided tour. Also visit the lesser-known **Recinte Modernista de Sant Pau** (p122) by Domènech i Montaner. For lunch, hit buzzy **Passeig de Sant Joan** (p131), **Tapas 24** (p126), **Betlem** (p127) or **Norte** (p129).

Explore more Modernisme along **Passeig de Gràcia** (pictured), including Gaudí's **Casa Batlló** (p116) and **La Pedrera** (p114). L'Eixample is full of fabulous shopping and rooftop bars.

Zip up to village-like Gràcia, with its lively **plazas** (p137), ecofriendly boutiques and **Mercat de la Llibertat** (p139). Grab vermouth and tapas at **Bodega Neus** (p144), or **La Vermu** (p144), or go for dinner at **La Pubilla** (p140) or **Lluritu** (p141).

Day 3

Time to take in the Mediterranean (pictured), perhaps with morning yoga or **paddle boarding** (p103). Then wander through Barceloneta, stopping at the **Mercat de la Barceloneta** (p97), **Bodega La Peninsular** (p103) or **La Cova Fumada** (p97).

Afterwards, explore the **Museu d'Història de Catalunya** (p100) or just relax at the **El Poblenou Platges** (p94).

Make your way over to reenergised El Poblenou. Meander along the cafe-dotted **Rambla del Poblenou** (p101) and its surrounding streets, where creative spots like the **Museu Can Framis** (p101) showcase the area's regeneration. Dine at **Can Recasens** (p102), **Els Pescadors** (p103) or **Can Fisher** (p102).

Day 4

Kick things off with a cable-car ride up to Montjuïc, then a stroll to the **Museu Nacional d'Art de Catalunya** (p160).

Wander down through Poble Sec, where **Palo Cortao** (p171), **La Platilleria** (p171), **Quimet i Quimet** (p170) and **Carrer de Blai** (p173) are foodie favourites. Hop across Avinguda del Paral·lel to trendy Sant Antoni, checking out the **Mercat de Sant Antoni** (p168).

Spend the evening soaking up bohemian El Raval. Catch an exhibition at the **MACBA** (pictured; architect: Richard Meier; p63) or an indie feature at the **Filmoteca de Catalunya** (p70). Finish with dinner at **Elisabets** (p61) or **Cañete** (p65) and cocktails at **Two Schmucks** (p68).

Need to Know

For detailed information, see Survival Guide (p177)

Language
Spanish, Catalan

Currency
Euro (€)

Visas
EU & Schengen countries No visa required.
UK, Australia, Canada, Israel, Japan, NZ & USA ETIAS pre-authorisation required from late 2023 (www.etiasvisa.com).
Other countries Check with local Spanish embassy.

Money
ATMs are widespread. Credit and debit cards are widely accepted.

Mobile Phones
Phones from within the EU have free roaming. Otherwise, your phone may support an e-sim with a data package. Local SIM cards work in most unlocked phones.

Time
Central European Time (GMT/UTC plus 1 hour)

Daily Budget

Budget: Less than €60
Dorm bed: €15–40
Set lunch: €12–15
Tapas/*pintxos:* €2–4 each
Bicycle hire per hour: €5

Midrange: €60–200
Standard double room: €80–170
Two-course dinner with wine: from €30
Guided tours and museum tickets: €15–40

Top end: More than €200
Double room in boutique and luxury hotels: from €170
Three-course meal at top restaurants: from €80
Concert tickets to Palau de la Música Catalana: around €45

Useful Websites

Barcelona (www.barcelona.cat) Town hall's site.

Barcelona Secreta (https://barcelonasecreta.com) Insider tips (in Spanish).

Barcelona Turisme (www.barcelonaturisme.com) City's official tourism board.

Foodie in Barcelona (www.foodieinbarcelona.com) Fab Barcelona food blog.

Lonely Planet (www.lonelyplanet.com/spain/barcelona) Destination information, hotel bookings, traveller forum and more.

Miniguide (https://miniguide.co) Style-conscious reviews and advice from locals.

Time Out Barcelona (www.timeout.com/barcelona) Restaurants and nightlife.

Arriving in Barcelona

✈ Aeroport de Barcelona–El Prat

Catch the frequent Aerobús into the city, (€5.90, 35 minutes; https://aerobusbarcelona.es), running 24 hours a day. Taxis cost around €30. Train and metro are also handy.

✈ Aeroport Girona–Costa Brava

Direct buses run to/from Barcelona's Estació del Nord bus station (€16, 1¼ hours).

✈ Aeroport de Reus

Buses run to/from the Estació d'Autobusos de Sants (€16, 1¾ hours).

🚌 Estació Sants

Long-distance trains arrive at this large station just west of the centre, which is linked by metro to other parts of the city. Some international buses arrive at the adjacent Estació d'Autobusos de Sants.

🚌 Estació d'Autobusos Barcelona Nord

Barcelona's main long-haul bus station is 1.5km northeast of Plaça de Catalunya, near the Arc de Triomf metro station in L'Eixample.

Getting Around

The excellent metro can get you most places, with buses and trams filling in the gaps. Single-ride tickets on all standard transport within Zone 1 cost €2.40; a 10-journey T-Casual ticket costs €11.35. Use taxis late at night.

Ⓜ Metro

Runs 5am to midnight Sunday to Thursday, to 2am Friday and 24 hours on Saturday.

🚌 Bus

Buses run frequently along most city routes from around 5am to around 11pm.

🚗 Taxi

Taxis are easily flagged down or booked by phone or app.

🚲 Bicycle

Barcelona has over 200km of bike lanes (with more on the way) and numerous bike-hire outlets.

🚠 Cable Car

Two cable cars zip up Montjuïc hill.

Barcelona Neighbourhoods

Gràcia & Park Güell (p133)
Lively, village-like Gràcia has vermouth bars, eco-boutiques and beautiful squares, all giving way to the Gaudí-designed wonderland of Park Güell.

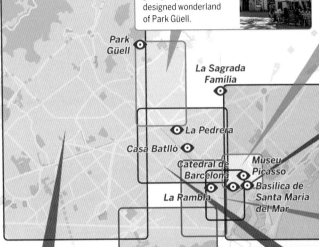

Park Güell ◉

La Sagrada Família ◉

◉ La Pedrera

Casa Batlló ◉

Catedral de Barcelona

Museu Picasso ◉

◉ ◉ ◉ Basílica de Santa Maria del Mar

La Rambla

Museu Nacional d'Art de Catalunya ◉ ◉ Fundació Joan Miró

Camp Nou, Pedralbes & La Zona Alta (p151)
A serene 14th-century monastery, hidden Gaudí treasures, superb dining, local hangouts in Sarrià and Sant Gervasi, and the pine-covered Collserola hills to escape into.

Montjuïc, Poble Sec & Sant Antoni (p159)
Montjuïc hosts wonderful museums, a formidable castle and colourful gardens, while Poble Sec and Sant Antoni are lively, restaurant-filled hangouts.

La Ribera & El Born (p73)

Splendid architecture, original boutiques, award-winning cocktail bars, fabulous tapas corners and the Museu Picasso await in this medieval corner of the Ciutat Vella.

The Barri Gòtic & La Rambla (p39)

Barcelona's old heart is a vision of medieval streets, monumental buildings, city bustle and centuries of history.

El Poblenou Beaches

Barceloneta, the Waterfront & El Poblenou (p93)

Explore the traditional 18th-century fishing quarter of Barceloneta, the sparkling golden beaches and the creative Poblenou neighbourhood.

El Raval (p59)

The city's most multicultural *barri* hosts ambitious art galleries, busy bars and restaurants, independent shops and a few cultural surprises.

L'Eixample & La Sagrada Família (p109)

Modernista treasures, broad boulevards, outstanding bars and restaurants, a shopping paradise and Gaudí galore.

Explore
Barcelona

Barcelona's Walking Tours

Plaça Reial (p45) MANUEL MILAN/SHUTTERSTOCK ©

Explore

The Barri Gòtic & La Rambla

Barcelona's original, labyrinthine core since Roman times, the Barri Gòtic is packed with historical treasures – relics of ancient Rome, Catalan Gothic churches and cobblestone lanes lined with bars, restaurants, galleries and shops. Extending along its western side, the famous La Rambla boulevard is always a hive of activity, packed with both tourists and locals, as well as historical jewels.

The Short List

○ **Catedral de Barcelona (p42)** *Exploring the spectacular cloister, shadowy chapels and nooks and crannies of this Catalan Gothic masterpiece.*

○ **Hidden Historical Treasures of the Barri Gòtic (p44)** *Enjoying a history walk before diving into the local food scene.*

○ **Museu d'Història de Barcelona (p48)** *Strolling the subterranean ruins of Roman Barcino and spotting the cathedral's foundations.*

○ **Mercat de la Boqueria (p49)** *Feasting on market-driven tapas and stocking up at fresh-produce stalls.*

○ **La Rambla (p40)** *Rising early to take in Barcelona's liveliest street scene.*

Getting There & Around

Ⓜ Key stops include Catalunya, Liceu, Drassanes, Jaume I and Urquinaona.

🚌 Airport and night buses arrive and depart from Plaça de Catalunya.

Neighbourhood Map on p46

Catedral de Barcelona (p42) MARIO MARCO/GETTY IMAGES ©

Top Experience

Dig into La Rambla's History

MAP P46, C6

Wedged between the Barri Gòtic and El Raval, Barcelona's most famous street is a window into Catalan culture and history. Flanked by plane trees, its middle section is a broad, always-crowded pedestrian boulevard. Though the busy tourist-centric scene won't appeal to everyone, a stroll here is pure sensory overload: churches, theatres and intriguing architecture mingle with souvenir hawkers, pavement artists and lively flower stalls.

History

La Rambla takes its name from a seasonal stream (*ramal* in Arabic) that once ran through here. Monastic buildings were then built, subsequently followed by the mansions of the well-to-do from the 16th to the early 19th centuries. Unofficially, La Rambla is divided into five sections, which explains why many people know it as Las Ramblas.

Pre-COVID, an estimated 78 million people visited each year. In late 2022, the city authorities began an extensive culture-focused overhaul of La Rambla, which will mean extra pavement space, reduced traffic and restoring the 17th-century Teatre Principal.

Highlights of La Rambla

The section immediately south of Plaça de Catalunya is **La Rambla de Canaletes**, which becomes **La Rambla dels Estudis**, overlooked by the baroque **Església de Betlem** and the neoclassical **Palau Moja** (https://patrimoni. gencat.cat). From Carrer de la Portaferrissa to Plaça de la Boqueria, what is officially called **La Rambla de Sant Josep** is lined with flower stalls. It's flanked on the west side by the lively Mercat de la Boqueria (p49), the 18th-century rococo **Palau de la Virreina** (https://ajuntament. barcelona.cat) and the Modernista bakery **Escribà** (www.escriba.es; 📶). At Plaça de la Boqueria, view the colourful 1976 pavement **mosaic** by Joan Miró; next to it, a 12m-long engraved **memorial** honours the 14 victims of the 2017 terrorist attack.

La Rambla dels Caputxins runs from Plaça de la Boqueria to Carrer dels Escudellers; on the western side is the Gran Teatre del Liceu (p55). Below this point La Rambla gets seedier as it becomes La Rambla de Santa Mónica, named for a convent that now hosts the **Centre d'Art Santa Mònica** (http://artssantamonica. gencat.cat).

★ Top Tips

o La Rambla is one of the most touristed spots in Barcelona, so swing by first thing in the morning to enjoy this historic leafy boulevard with reduced crowds.

o Bear in mind that some areas of La Rambla (particularly the southern part) can be dodgy after dark.

o Keep an eye on your belongings, wear backpacks on your front and be aware that pickpockets abound.

✖ Take a Break

Duck into El Raval for speciality coffee and delectable tapas at Bar Central (p65) or a classic Catalan meal at long-running Elisabets (p61).

Alternatively, grab a coffee at **Café de l'Òpera** (www. cafeoperabcn.com; 📶) or one of the many restaurants that line Plaça Reial (p45).

Top Experience 📷

Marvel at the Magnificent Catedral de Barcelona

Rising above the Barri Gòtic's alleys, Barcelona's central place of worship presents a spectacular image. The richly decorated main facade, dotted with gargoyles and the kinds of intricacies you would expect of northern European Gothic, sets it apart from other Barcelona churches. Most of the building dates between 1298 and 1460, though the facade was added between 1887 and 1890.

◎ MAP P46, D3

www.catedralbcn.org

Interior & Roof

Built on the site of a Romanesque predecessor, the cathedral has a broad, soaring interior divided into a central nave and two aisles by lines of elegant, slim pillars in classic Catalan Gothic style. It was one of the few churches in Barcelona spared by the anarchists in the civil war, so its ornamentation, never overly lavish, is intact. In the middle of the central nave is the exquisitely sculpted late-14th-century timber *coro* (choir stalls). A broad staircase before the main altar leads to the crypt, which contains the 14th-century tomb of Santa Eulàlia, one of Barcelona's two patron saints.

Apart from the cathedral's main facade, the rest is sparsely decorated, and the two octagonal, flat-roofed towers confirm that even here, Catalan Gothic architectural principles prevailed.

Cloister

From the southwest transept, exit by the white-marble Romanesque door next to the coffins of Count Ramon Berenguer I and his wife Almodis, founders of the original 11th-century Romanesque church. Enter the leafy *claustre* (cloister), with its tinkling fountains and whispering palm trees; the flock of 13 geese supposedly represents the age of Santa Eulàlia at the time of her martyrdom and have, generation after generation, been squawking here since medieval days. The Capella de Santa Llúcia is one of the few remnants of Romanesque Barcelona, though its interior is largely Gothic.

Casa de l'Ardiaca

Opposite the cathedral, the serene 16th-century **Casa de l'Ardiaca** (https://ajuntament. barcelona.cat) has housed the city's archives since the 1920s and was renovated by Lluís Domènech i Montaner in 1902. The original 12th-century building was built using part of the old Roman wall, which you can still see on the lower northwest side.

★ Top Tips

o Although technically it's free to go into the cathedral to pray, in practice, if you go any time during tourist visiting hours, you'll need to pay.

o At 6pm Saturday and 11am Sunday, *sardanes* (traditional Catalan dances) are performed in the square in front of the cathedral.

o For a bird's-eye view, zip up to the rooftop by lift from the Capella dels Sant Innocents.

✕ Take a Break

Head to Placeta de Manuel Ribé, where Levante (p52) does delectable Mediterranean–Middle Eastern cuisine and Brugarol (p50) fuses Japanese and Catalan flavours to perfection.

Or grab a paper cone of piping-hot *xurros* (churros in Spanish) at takeaway-only **Xurreria** (Carrer dels Banys Nous 8).

Walking Tour 🚶

Hidden Historical Treasures of the Barri Gòtic

This scenic walk through the Barri Gòtic will take you back in time, from the early days of Roman-era Barcino through to medieval times. The 20th century has also left its mark here, from the tragic scars of the Spanish Civil War to artistic contributions.

Walk Facts

Start Col·legi d'Arquitectes; Ⓜ Jaume I, Liceu

End Plaça del Rei; Ⓜ Jaume I

Length 1.8km; two hours

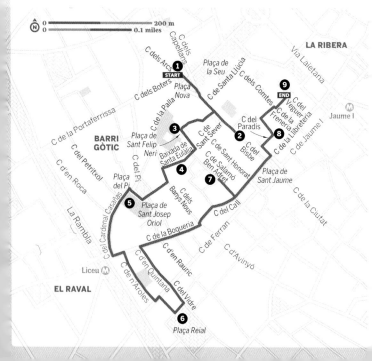

❶ Picasso

Start by admiring the facade of the 1931 **Col·legi de Arquitectes** (https://arquitectes.cat), opposite the cathedral. This giant 1962 contribution by Picasso represents Mediterranean festivals, including Catalonia's *castellers* (human-tower performers).

❷ Pont del Bisbe

This Gothic-style marble bridge, linking the Palau de la Generalitat with the Casa dels Canonges, may look centuries old, but it was, in fact, created in the 1920s by Modernista architect Joan Rubió i Bellver.

❸ Plaça de Sant Felip Neri

On this acacia-shaded square, damaged by pro-Francoist bombers in 1938, a plaque com-memorates the 42 victims (mostly children) who died there.

❹ Santa Eulàlia

On the slender lane of Baixada de Santa Eulàlia, you'll spot a small **statue of Santa Eulàlia**, one of Barcelona's patron saints, who suffered various tortures during her martyrdom.

❺ Basílica de Santa Maria del Pi

The looming 14th-century Ba-sílica de Santa Maria del Pi (www.basilicadelpi.cat) is famed for its magnificent rose window and clas-sic Catalan Gothic lines. Outside, the two squares flanking the basilica are some of the prettiest in Barcelona, awash with art and food markets.

❻ Plaça Reial

Zigzag south to arcaded Plaça Reial, one of Barcelona's liveliest squares, with its 19th-century neo-classical buildings. The lampposts by the fountain are Antoni Gaudí's first known works in the city.

❼ Sinagoga Major

Follow Carrer de Salomó Ben Adret into El Call, once the heart of Barcelona's Jewish quarter, until the bloody pogrom of 1391. The Sinagoga Major (p50), one of Europe's oldest, was discovered in 1996. Tiny **Placeta de Manuel Ribé** is a lovely spot for a break.

❽ Roman Temple

On Carrer del Paradís you'll pass the unassuming entrance to the **Temple d'August** (www.barcelona.cat/museuhistoria): four Roman columns hidden in an intriguing building with Gothic and baroque touches, on the highest point of Roman Barcino.

❾ Plaça del Rei

Your final stop is grand Plaça del Rei, where the Reyes Católicos (Catholic Monarchs) received Co-lumbus following his first voyage to the Americas. The former palace today houses the superb **Museu d'Història de Barcelona**.

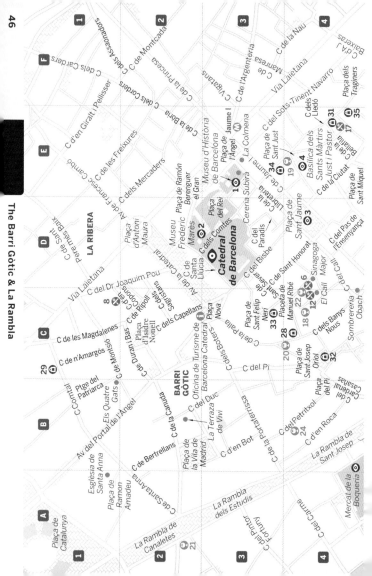

The Barri Gòtic & La Rambla

The Barri Gòtic & La Rambla

C de la Fusteria

5

C de Marquet

C de la Plata 9
Pla de la Mercè 10
C Ample 11 Simó Rooftop Olter at Serras 6

C d'en Gignàs 13

Porta de Mar

C del Regomir

C d'Atauif

Milans C Ample

15 14 C de la Comtessa de Sobradiel

27

C dels Templers

C del Palau

C de George Orwell

C de Cervantes C d'Avinyó

Baixada de Sant Miquel

30

C de la Lleona

C dels Escudellers Blancs C de n' Àgla

23

C del Vidre

Plaça Reial

26 C Nou de Zurbano

C de n'Aroles

C d'en Quintana

16

C de la Boqueria

Plaça de la Boqueria

Liceu

El Quim
Direkte Boqueria
EL RAVAL

Joan La Llar del Pernil

C de l'Arc de Sant Agustí

C del Marquès de Barberà

C de Sant Pau

Plaça de Sant Agustí

C de la Junta de Comerç

C de l'Hospital

Plaça de Salvador Seguí

C d'en Robador

La Rambla de la Unió

La Rambla dels Caputxins

25

La Rambla

C de les Penedides

C Nou de la Rambla

C de Lancaster

C de l'Arc del Teatre

C de la Guàrdia

C de l'Est

C de Montserrat

Drassanes

C del Portal Santa Madrona

La Rambla de Santa Mònica

Plaça del Teatre

Plaça de Joaquim Xirau

Ptge de la Pau

C Nou de Sant Francesc 7

C d'en Rull

C dels Còdols

C d'en Serra

C de la Mercè

Plaça de la Mercè

Plaça del Duc de Medinaceli

5 Basílica de la Mercè 6

Pg de Colom

C de Josep Anselm Clavé C del Parc

Ronda del Litoral

Moll de la Fusta

Port de Barcelona

200 m
0.1 miles

For reviews see	
◆ Top Experiences	p40
◎ Sights	p48
✕ Eating	p50
◑ Drinking	p53
✪ Entertainment	p55
ⓐ Shopping	p55

Sights

Museu d'Història de Barcelona

MUSEUM

1 ⊙ MAP P46, E3

One of Barcelona's most fascinating museums travels back through the centuries to the very foundations of Roman Barcino. You'll stroll through 4 sq km of excavated Roman and Visigothic Barcelona, among the old streets, sewers, laundries, baths and wine- and fish-making factories that flourished here following the town's founding by Emperor Augustus around 10 BCE. Equally impressive is the building itself, which was once part of the Palau Reial Major (Grand Royal Palace) on Plaça del Rei (p45), among the key locations of medieval princely power in Barcelona. (MUHBA; www.barcelona.cat/museuhistoria)

Museu Frederic Marès

MUSEUM

2 ⊙ MAP P46, D2

The wealthy Catalan sculptor, traveller and collector Frederic Marès i Deulovol (1893–1991) amassed an astonishing collection of historical curios, particularly medieval Spanish sculptures. Today, his displays of religious art and antiques (which he donated to the city) await inside this vast medieval complex, once part of the royal palace of the counts of Barcelona, then later the seat of the Spanish Inquisition in Barcelona. (www.barcelona.cat/museufredericmares)

Plaça de Sant Jaume

SQUARE

3 ⊙ MAP P46, D4

In the 2000 or so years since the Romans settled here, the area around this often-remodelled square, which started life as the forum, has been the focus of Barcelona's civic life – and it's still the central staging area for Barcelona's traditional festivals. Facing each other across the square are the **Palau de la Generalitat** (http://presidencia.gencat.cat), the seat of Catalonia's regional government, on the north side, and Barcelona's **Ajuntament** (Casa de la Ciutat; www.bcn.cat) on the south.

Basílica dels Sants Màrtirs Just i Pastor

CHURCH

4 ⊙ MAP P46, E4

This slightly neglected single-nave church, with chapels on either side of the buttressing, was built in 1342 in Catalan Gothic style on what is reputedly the site of the oldest parish church in Barcelona. Climb the bell tower for knockout views. (www.basilicasantjust.cat)

Basilica de la Mercè

CHURCH

5 ⊙ MAP P46, F6

Raised in the 1760s on the site of its Gothic predecessor, this baroque church is home to Barcelona's most celebrated patron saint. Though it was badly damaged during the Spanish Civil War, what remains is quite a curiosity. (www.basilicadelamerce.cat)

Grabbing a Bargain at Mercat de la Boqueria

Barcelona's most central fresh-produce market, the **Mercat de la Boqueria** (Map p46, B4; www.boqueria.barcelona), is one of Spain's greatest sound, smell and colour sensations. It's housed in a packed-out Modernista-influenced building constructed between 1840 and 1914 under architect Josep Mas i Vila, on the site of the former Sant Josep monastery on the west side of La Rambla. There is believed to have been a market on this spot since 1217, and as much as La Boqueria has become a modern-day attraction, some *barcelonins* do still try to shop here (usually early on), including top restaurateurs. What is now known as La Boqueria didn't come to exist until the 19th century, with the iron Modernista gate added in 1914.

In recent years, La Boqueria has taken a tourist-oriented turn and become extremely overcrowded, though towards the back you can still discover what it's really about: bountiful fruit and vegetables, and seemingly limitless sea critters, cheeses and meats. When tourism came to a halt during the COVID-19 pandemic, the enterprising stallholders turned to home deliveries and online orders, and there is hope that going forward, the market will attract more local shoppers as well as visitors. It's a good idea to ask permission before taking stallholders' pictures and always try to buy something from their stall.

It's also worth bearing in mind that Barcelona has almost 40 fabulous markets, all stuffed with fresh produce and offering a few bars and restaurants at which to sample local specialities – such as the **Mercat de Sant Antoni** (p168), Gràcia's **Mercat de la Llibertat** (p139) and L'Eixample's **Mercat de la Concepció** (p122). Within La Boqueria, pull up a stool at **El Quim** (Map p46, B5; www.facebook.com/elquimdelaboqueria) for traditional, market-fresh Catalan dishes, including fried eggs with baby squid, or soak up the clamour over classic cooking at **Bar Pinotxo** (www.pinotxobar.com), standing strong since 1940. **Direkte Boqueria** (Map p46, B5; www.direkte.cat), with just eight bar seats, is popular for chef Arnau Muñío's creative fusion of Catalan ingredients and Asian flavours. Among the many piled-high counters, family-owned **Joan La Llar del Pernil** (Map p46. A5; www.joanlallardelpernil.com) sells some of the city's best *pernil* (cured ham; *jamón* in Spanish).

Visiting
Atmospheric El Call

One of the most atmospheric parts of the Ciutat Vella is El Call (pronounced 'kye'), the medieval Jewish quarter that flourished here until a tragic 14th-century pogrom. Today its narrow lanes conceal what some historians consider to be the city's main medieval **synagogue** (Map p46, D4; www.sinagogamayor.com) and the remains of the Jewish weaver Jucef Bonhiac's **house** (Map p46, C4; www.barcelona.cat/museuhistoria; Placeta de Manuel Ribé). The boundaries of the **Call Major** are roughly Carrer del Call, Carrer dels Banys Nous, Baixada de Santa Eulàlia and Carrer de Sant Honorat; another pocket, the **Call Menor**, extended across the modern Carrer de Ferran as far as Baixada de Sant Miquel and Carrer d'en Rauric.

Eating

Brugarol   FUSION €€€

6 ⊗ MAP P46, D4

Taking inspiration from Japan's izakaya bars, intimate Brugarol wows with its creative fusion tapas that change with the seasons. Most of the all-organic ingredients come from the Costa Brava, including artisanal cheeses, natural wines and olive oil from the owners' farms. Irresistible dishes include tuna-tartare wonton, *corvina* sashimi and truffle flan with shiitake. There's a second branch in L'Eixample (p126). (www.brugarolbarcelona.com)

La Vinateria
del Call   SPANISH €€

In a magical, rambling setting in the ancient Jewish quarter, just across the alley from Brugarol (see 6 ⊗ Map p46, D4), this tiny candlelit jewel-box of a wine bar serves up divine Iberian sharing plates roaming from Galician-style octopus and *botifarra* (sausage) from Vic to perfect *truites* (omelettes). Boasting spot-on service, super-fresh local ingredients and a wonderful selection of wines and artisan cheeses from across Spain. (www.lavinateriadelcall.com; 🛜)

Federal   CAFE €

7 ⊗ MAP P46, E7

With brick-walled industrial-chic design and tables on a palm-studded square, this welcoming (and pet-friendly) branch of Barcelona's beloved Aussie-founded Federal (p170) serves local-produce brunches and perfectly poured flat whites to a lively international crowd. It's known for deliciously original bites such as shakshouka with labneh. (www.federalcafe.es; 🛜)

Koy Shunka

JAPANESE €€€

8  MAP P46, C1

Down a narrow lane north of the cathedral, chef Hideki Matsuhisa's Michelin-starred Koy Shunka opens a portal to sensational dishes from the East – mouth-watering sushi, sashimi, seared Wagyu beef and richly flavoured seaweed salads are served alongside inventive fusion specialities, most rooted in Mediterranean ingredients. Don't miss the signature tender tuna belly. (www.koyshunka.com)

Bar La Plata

TAPAS €

9  MAP P46, F6

Hidden away near the waterfront, tile-walled La Plata is a humble, well-loved bodega that has served just four simple, perfect plates since launching back in 1945: *pescadito frito* (fried fish), *botifarra* (sausage), anchovies, and tomato salad. Throw in drinkable, affordable wines and vermouth. (www.barlaplata.com)

Informal

CATALAN €€€

10  MAP P46, F6

Celebrated chef Marc Gascons, who won a Michelin star with Els Tinars near Girona, is behind the smartly laid-back restaurant at the uber-chic hotel Serras. Classic Catalan favourites such as grilled-prawn *arrós* (rice), chicken-filled *canelons* (Catalan-style cannelloni) and chargrilled turbot are given a contemporary twist. Up on the rooftop, pair crafted cocktails with waterfront views. (https://restauranteinformal.com)

The Barri Gòtic & La Rambla Eating

Plaça Reial (p45)

Bar Celta
GALICIAN €

11 MAP P46, F6

Founded by a Galician couple in 1970 and still in the family, charmingly fuss-free Bar Celta shows off the northwestern region's famously seafood-tastic culinary riches with its house *pop a feira* (Galician-style octopus). Other traditional home-cooked goodies include salty Padrón peppers, *patates braves* and giant wedges of tortilla. There's another branch (p88) in El Born. (www.barcelta.com)

Levante
MEDITERRANEAN €€

12 MAP P46, C4

A stylish, snug space tucked into the old Call, Levante specialises in

Els Quatre Gats

Once the lair of Barcelona's Modernista artists, **Els Quatre Gats** (Map p46, B1; www.4gats.com) is a stunning example of the movement, with its colourful patterned tiles, geometric brickwork and wooden fittings designed by Josep Puig i Cadafalch. It was here, in 1900, that Pablo Picasso held his first solo exhibition. The local-focused cuisine (grilled meats and rice dishes) isn't as thrilling as the setting, but you can just pop in for coffee.

beautifully prepped sharing plates that delicately blend Mediterranean and Middle Eastern flavours: spicy roast-carrot salad, coriander-infused shakshouka, and zesty hummus with pomegranate. Dangling plants grace the interior, and natural wines abound. (www.bistrotlevante.com;)

Milk
INTERNATIONAL €

13 MAP P46, F5

Also loved for its crafted cocktails, Irish-run Milk rescues Barcelona night owls with morning-after brunches (until 4.30pm!). Arrive early or join the wait list for lemon-dusted avocado toast, banana pancakes, egg-white omelettes stuffed with *piquillo* peppers and more. The same team runs L'Eixample's Firebug and Gigi von Tapas. (www.milkbarcelona.com;)

Koku Ramen
RAMEN €

14 MAP P46, E6

Homemade noodles and gyoza, local Catalan ingredients and traditional Japanese recipes make pioneering Koku one of Barcelona's most popular ramen spots. Vegetarian temptations revolve around steaming shiitake-and-kombu broths. Also in El Born (p87). (https://kokukitchen.es)

La Pachuca
MEXICAN €

15 MAP P46, E6

The sister *taquería* to El Raval's forever-packed, Mexican-owned

El Pachuco (p65) delivers its signature margaritas, mezcals and home-cooked, market-driven tacos and quesadillas with authentically delicious flair. Try the chicken-and-*mole* tacos, zingy guac or corn-truffle quesadillas. (www.facebook.com/LaPachucaBcn)

Can Culleretes

CATALAN €€

16 MAP P46, C5

Founded in 1786, Barcelona's oldest restaurant is still going strong, with visitors and locals alike flocking here for its rambling interior, old-fashioned tile-filled decor and enormous helpings of straightforward traditional Catalan food. Specialities include fresh seafood, grilled meats, steaming stews and stuffed *canelons*. (www.culleretes. com; 🛜)

Capet

CATALAN €€

17 MAP P46, E4

Rooted in the freshest produce, this elegant Gràcia-born restaurant delivers a contemporary spin on traditional Catalan cuisine from its open-plan bistro-style kitchen. The short-but-sweet seasonal menu, with a South American touch courtesy of Venezuelan chef Armando Álvarez, might include duck-laced rice, cod in *pil pil* (garlic, chilli and oil) sauce and zingy salads of tomato, peach, sardines and ricotta. (http://capetrestaurant.com)

Roman Walls

From Plaça del Rei it's worth a detour to see the two best surviving stretches of Barcelona's Roman walls, which once boasted 78 towers. One section is on the southern side of **Plaça de Ramon Berenguer el Gran**, with the 14th-century **Capella Reial de Santa Àgata** atop. Another piece of wall sits towards the northern end of Carrer del Sots-Tinent Navarro, while more can be seen at the **Porta de Mar** (Map p46, E5; www. barcelona.cat/museuhistoria) archaeological site.

Drinking

Satan's Coffee Corner

COFFEE

18 MAP P46, C4

All ocean-blue walls, pounding beats and punk-inspired style overlooking a leafy plaza, Satan's is firmly about the coffee (no laptops!). Local small-scale roaster Right Side provides regularly rotating signature brews, while snazzy snacks include Japanese-influenced breakfasts. There's also a branch in L'Eixample (p128). (www.satanscoffee.com)

The Barri Gòtic & La Rambla Drinking

Rooftop Bars

La Terraza de Vivi (Map p46, B2; www.kimptonvividorahotel. com) Wraparound views and crafted cocktails at the Kimpton Vividora.

Serras (Map p46, F6; https:// serrashotel.com) Dreamy hotel rooftop for creative cocktails, with fabulous cuisine by chef Marc Gascons.

Bar Zim   WINE BAR

19 🚇 MAP P46, E4

A teensy, intimate, cavern-like bar where Catalan (Penedès, Empordà) and lesser-known Spanish wines take centre stage below beamed ceilings. Pair with one of the delicate platters of local cheeses or cold cuts with artisan jams.

Caelum   CAFE

20 🚇 MAP P46, C4

Centuries of heavenly Spanish gastronomic tradition collide at this exquisite medieval space in the heart of the city that stocks sweets made by nuns across the country. The ground-floor cafe is a soothing setting for cakes and pastries, and in the stone-walled underground chamber, flickering candles cast a glow on a ruined medieval bath-house. (www.facebook.com/CaelumBarcelona; 🛜 👫)

Bar Boadas   COCKTAIL BAR

21 🚇 MAP P46, A2

One of Barcelona's oldest cocktail bars, Boadas is famed for its daiquiris. Amid old monochrome photos and a polished-wood bar, bow-tied waiters have been mixing unique, deliciously drinkable creations since Miguel Boadas opened it in 1933 – Miró and Hemingway both drank here. (www. boadascocktails.com)

Čaj Chai   TEAHOUSE

22 🚇 MAP P46, C4

Inspired by Prague's bohemian tearooms, this bright and buzzing temple to steaming brews in the heart of the old Jewish quarter is a much-loved local haunt. Pick from around 200 world-roaming organic teas, plus fresh cakes and pastries from local bakers. (www. cajchai.com)

Marula Café   CLUB

23 🚇 MAP P46, D6

The Barri Gòtic outpost of a Madrid-born nightlife sensation, Marula transports you to the 1970s and the best in funk and soul. DJs slip in other tunes too, and there are regular live gigs. (www.marulacafe.com)

Granja La Pallaresa   CAFE

24 🚇 MAP P46, B4

On the Barri Gòtic's 'Chocolate Street', old-school La Pallaresa dates back to the 1940s and pulls in both locals and visitors with its crispy *xurros*, impossible-to-resist pastries and *ensaïmades* (Balearic-style sweet buns) from Mallorca. ()

Entertainment

Gran Teatre del Liceu THEATRE

25 ⭐ MAP P46, B6

Barcelona's grand old opera house, skilfully restored after a fire in 1994, is one of the world's most technologically advanced theatres. Catch a show in its grand auditorium, returned to all its 19th-century glory but with the very latest in acoustics, or join a guided tour to explore its architectural beauty. (www. liceubarcelona.cat)

Jamboree LIVE MUSIC

26 ⭐ MAP P46, C6

For over half a century, Jamboree has been bringing joy to Barcelona's jivers, with high-calibre acts featuring jazz trios, blues, Afrobeats, Latin and big-band sounds; big names such as Chet Baker and Ornette Coleman have graced the stage here. After midnight, it morphs into a DJ-spinning club. (https://jamboreejazz.com)

Harlem Jazz Club JAZZ

27 ⭐ MAP P46, E5

This narrow, old-city dive is one of the best spots in town for jazz, as well as funk, Latin, blues and

gypsy jazz, and attracts a mixed crowd that maintains a respectful silence during performances. Get in early for a front-row seat. (www. harlemjazzclub.es)

Shopping

L'Arca FASHION & ACCESSORIES

28 🔒 MAP P46, C4

Step inside this enchanting vintage boutique for beautifully crafted apparel from the past: 18th-century embroidered silk vests, elaborate silk kimonos and 1920s shawls and wedding dresses, plus old-style earrings made by artisans in southern Spain. The incredible collection has provided fashion for films like *Titanic*. (https://larcabarcelona.com)

Raima STATIONERY

29 🔒 MAP P46, C1

Spread across a 15th-century building, and family-owned since 1986, Raima is a wonderland of trinkets for writing, painting, illustrating and more. Walls are decorated with paper-made flowers and dresses. (https://raima.cat)

La Manual Alpargatera SHOES

30 🔒 MAP P46, D5

Stars from Penélope Cruz to Jean Paul Gaultier have ordered personalised *espardenyes* (espadrilles) from this famous shoe specialist founded in 1940. (https://lamanual.com)

Le Swing
FASHION & ACCESSORIES

31 MAP P46, E4

Specialising in haute-couture classics like Chanel, Dior, Givenchy and Yves Saint Laurent, collected from Paris and LA as well as Barcelona, this sparkling stone-walled boutique is a temple to designer vintage and neovintage fashion from the 1920s onwards. (www.leswingvintage.com)

Mostra d'Art Pintors del Pi
MARKET

32 MAP P46, C4

For over 40 years, local artists have each weekend been setting up stalls outside the 14th-century Basílica de Santa Maria del Pi (p45). They're often joined, on the adjacent Plaça del Pi, by the **Col·lectiu d'Artesans de l'Alimentació market**, devoted to artisanal Catalan food products (olive oil, vermouth, honey and marmalade). (www.pintorspibarcelona.com)

Sabater Hermanos
COSMETICS

33 MAP P46, C3

Handcrafted, biodegradable soaps and soap petals in seductive flavours like olive oil, cinnamon and orange blossom are the draw at this fragrant little shop set within an old textiles factory, where every product is both cruelty-free and vegan. (www.sabaterhnos.com)

La Rambla (p40)

Preserving Barcelona's Historic Shops

From centuries-old candle-makers to family bakeries, Barcelona's traditional, historical, specialist shops are just as essential to the city's soul as Gaudí's Modernista creations. Over the last few years, however, some of the best-known shops have been forced to close, largely down to rising rents (in some cases linked to growing numbers of tourist apartments pushing up prices) and the worldwide closures caused by the COVID-19 pandemic. In 2015, 228 businesses across Barcelona were given a special preservation status, which means that their original facades and interiors can't be altered, though many have still been forced to shutter since. It's estimated that the average age among Barcelona's shops is less than 19 years, which means traditional businesses sadly continue to decrease.

Visitors can show their support by shopping at much-loved Barcelona icons such as bakeries **Escribà** (p41) and **La Colmena** (Map p46, E3; www.pastisserialacolmena.com), hat-maker **Sombrerería Obach** (Map p46, C4; www.sombreriaobach.es), candle-producer **Cerería Subirà** (Map p46, E3; https://cereriasubira.cat) and dried-fruit specialist **Casa Gispert** (p91), or dining at protected restaurants such as **Can Culleretes** (p53), **Bar Muy Buenas** (p61) and **7 Portes** (p104).

Casa Carot   CHEESE

34 MAP P46, E3

A former 20th-century butter factory has been beautifully transformed into an irresistible cheese haven devoted to small-producer Catalan products that prioritise animal rights. Collserola honey, Poblenou gin, local marmalade, natural wines and fresh-baked bread also fill the shelves.

Roberto & Victoria   JEWELLERY

35 MAP P46, E4

Jeweller duo Roberto Carrascosa and Victoria Aroca handcraft exquisite, unique pieces in gold, silver, brass and semiprecious stones at their minimalist studio, combining avant-garde touches with classic design and reworking vintage jewels into contemporary 'cult jewellery'. (www.roberto-victoria.com)

Explore ◈
El Raval

The once down-and-out district of El Raval is one of Barcelona's most vibrant and multicultural neighbourhoods. Though still seedy in parts, it has seen remarkable rejuvenation in recent years, with cutting-edge galleries (such as MACBA), arty cafes, creative boutiques and trendy restaurants dotted among the food shops, historical bars and ancient relics. What El Raval lacks in blockbuster sights it makes up for with louche charm, good food and intriguing corners.

The Short List

○ **MACBA (p63)** Getting to grips with the occasionally challenging art collection and watching skaters perform their tricks out the front.

○ **Dinner time (p65)** Diving into Barcelona's most multicultural food scene, from classic Catalan at Elisabets to tacos at El Pachuco and Bacaro's Italian delights.

○ **Palau Güell (p63)** Wandering around this artfully restored palace, an early Gaudí masterpiece.

○ **Bar scene (p68)** Seeking out avant-garde cocktails at stylish dens like Two Schmucks and La Confieria.

○ **Street art (p64)** Learning all about Barcelona's lively street art and graffiti hub on an artist-led walking tour.

Getting There

Ⓜ Línies 1, 2 and 3 stop at strategic points around El Raval, so nothing is far from the metro. Liceu, Sant Antoni, Catalunya and Drassanes are handy stops.

Neighbourhood Map on p62

MACBA (p63); architect: Richard Meier GIMAS/SHUTTERSTOCK ©

Walking Tour 🚶

Revelling in El Raval

El Raval is a neighbourhood whose contradictory impulses are legion. This journey through the local life of the barri takes you from tradition-inspired haunts beloved by the savvy young professionals moving into the area to gritty streetscapes and timeworn taverns. Unlike much of the neighbourhood, the stops along the route have barely changed in decades.

Walk Facts

Start Kasparo; Ⓜ Universitat, Ⓜ Catalunya

End Bar El Pollo; Ⓜ Universitat, Ⓜ Urgell

Length 1.5km; half a day

❶ Kasparo

This friendly terrace **cafe** (www.kasparo.es; 🛜), overlooking a traffic-free square from beneath the arches, is a neighbourhood favourite for juices, salads, creative *entrepans* (rolls) and tasty tapas.

❷ Elisabets

Northern El Raval is rapidly gentrifying, but places like brilliant Elisabets, loved for its good-value cooking, bring a taste of traditional Barcelona. The *menú del dia* changes daily; you can also try typical tapas like *botifarra* (Catalan sausage) or *fuet* (thin pork sausage).

❸ La Portorriqueña

Coffee beans from around the world, freshly ground before your eyes, have been the winning formula since 1902 at La Portorriqueña (https://cafeselmagnifico.com), now run by the team behind Barcelona's beloved Cafés El Magnífico. Carrer d'en Xuclà is good for little old-fashioned food boutiques.

❹ Granja M Viader

For over a century, people have been coming to classically Catalan milk bar Granja M Viader for hot chocolate ladled out with whipped cream (ask for a *suís*). It also sells cheeses, cakes and charcuterie.

❺ Antic Hospital de la Santa Creu

Dip into the peaceful, orange-scented courtyard gardens of the 15th-century **hospital** (p64) where Antoni Gaudí spent his final moments; it now hosts the Biblioteca de Catalunya.

❻ Bar Muy Buenas

Now serving impressive cocktails and typical Catalan dishes, Modernista classic Muy Buenas (http://muybuenas.cat) has been a bar since 1928 and wears its past proudly with stunning original woodwork, etched windows and a marble bar. It's one of Barcelona's officially protected heritage buildings (p57).

❼ Carrer de la Riera Baixa

Famed for its wealth of second-hand shops, Riera Baixa hosts its own lively vintage market each Saturday.

❽ Casa Almirall

In business since 1860 on now-trendy Carrer de Joaquín Costa, corner bar Casa Almirall (www.casaalmirall.com; 🛜) is dark and intriguing, with Modernista decor, a mixed clientele, and absinthe and vermouth (including the signature *oliveta*) on the menu.

❾ Bar El Pollo

Delectable tortillas line up on the metallic bar at Basque-run El Pollo, an everyday neighbourhood tapas bar since 1987, now given fresh energy.

El Raval

L'EIXAMPLE

C de Balmes

A

C de les Corts Catalanes

Rambla de Catalunya

B

Pg de Gràcia

Catalunya

Plaça de Catalunya

C

D

For reviews see
- ◉ Sights — p63
- 🍴 Eating — p65
- 🍷 Drinking — p68
- ✪ Entertainment — p70
- 🔒 Shopping — p70

1

Universitat de Barcelona

Gran Via de les Corts Catalanes

Ronda de la Universitat

Oficina d'Informació de Turisme de Barcelona
Plaça de Catalunya

BARRI GÒTIC

C de Santa Anna

C de la Canuda

Plaça Nova

2

A1 & A2 Aerobús

Ⓜ Universitat **16** ✪

C de Pelai

Plaça de Vicenç Martorell

Ⓜ Catalunya

C de Bergara

Flamingos Vintage Kilo

C de la Portaferrissa

C dels Tallers

Holala! Plaza

21

C de les Ramelleres

23 C del Bonsuccés

La Rambla

Centre de Cultura Contemporània de Barcelona

C del Doctor Dou

◉**7** ✪

C d'Elisabets

17 ◉ ◉**19**

Negroni

Lucky Schmuck

🔒**34**

5

MACBA ◉**1**

Plaça dels Àngels

33 🔒 **32** ✪

31 🔒

C del Pintor Fortuny

C d'en Xuclà

Montalegre

3

Ronda de Sant Antoni

30 🔒

18 **29** ✪

14 ✪

12 ✪

C del Notariat

C de Jerusalem

Mercat de la Boqueria

C de la Boqueria

C del Peu de la Creu

C de Joaquín Costa

C del Lleó

C de la Lluna

Plaça del Pes de la Palla

🔒**28** 33 | 45

C del Carme

C de les Egipcíaques

Antic Hospital de la Santa Creu

◉**4**

✪**13**

Liceu Ⓜ

C de Ferran

EL RAVAL

C de la Riera Alta

C de l'Hospital

4

✪**27**

11 C de Sant ✪ Antoni Abat

Ⓜ Sant Antoni

Plaça del Pedró

Rambla del Raval

◉**3**

C d'en Robador

C de la Junta de Comerç

C de Sant Pau

Plaça de Salvador Seguí

22 🍴

✪**26**

C del Marquès de Barberà

✪**8**

Plaça Reial

La Rambla

Palau Güell

◉**2**

5

SANT ANTONI

Ronda de Sant Pau

C del Comte Borrell

C de la Cera

C de les Carretes

C de la Riereta

C de la Reina Amàlia

Plaça de Josep Maria Folch i Torres

✪**10**

25 ✪

C de Sant Pau

9

C de Sant Pau

C de Sant Oleguer

15 ✪

🔒**24**

C de l'Arc del Teatre

Drassanes Ⓜ

C Nou de la Rambla

C de les Tàpies

Av de les Drassanes

C de l'Om

C de l'Arc del Teatre

C del Portal/Santa Madrona

El Flea

🍴**20**

◉**6**

Església de Sant Pau del Camp

C d'Aldana

Av del Paral·lel

POBLE SEC

Ⓜ Paral·lel

Av del Paral·lel

C de Cabanes

Jardins de les Tres Xemeneies

C Nou de la Rambla

C de Vila i Vila

C de Palaudàries

6

N 0 ____ 200 m
0 ____ 0.1 miles

A

B

C

D

Sights

MACBA
GALLERY

1 MAP P62, B3

An extraordinary all-white, glass-fronted creation by American architect Richard Meier, opened in 1995, the MACBA is the city's foremost contemporary art centre, with captivating exhibitions for the serious art lover. The permanent collection is dedicated to Spanish and Catalan art from the 1960s to the present day, with works by Antoni Tàpies, Joan Brossa, Miquel Barceló, Eduardo Chillida, Mari Chordà, Joan Rabascall and Concha Jerez. International artists, such as Paul Klee, Bruce Nauman, Alexander Calder, John Cage and Jean-Michel Basquiat,

are also represented. (Museu d'Art Contemporani de Barcelona; www.macba.cat)

Palau Güell
PALACE

2 MAP P62, D4

Built off La Rambla in the late 1880s for Gaudí's wealthy patron, the industrialist Eusebi Güell, the Unesco-protected Palau Güell is a magnificent example of the early days of the architect's fevered architectural imagination. This extraordinary neo-Gothic mansion (one of the few major buildings of that era raised in the Ciutat Vella) gives an insight into its maker's prodigious genius, and, though sombre compared with later whims, it's a characteristic riot of styles (Gothic, Islamic, art nouveau) and materials. Highlights

Palau Güell

Street Art in El Raval

Since Barcelona's street-art scene kicked off in the 1970s, El Raval has grown into its epicentre. Beside the **MACBA** (p63), Keith Haring's 1989 *Todos juntos podemos parar el SIDA*, which played an important role in destigmatising HIV and AIDS in Spain, is El Raval's best-known open-air piece. Other highlights include the many scattered Me Lata installations, created using tin cans hand-scrawled with messages of love, and Carlos Redón's dummy logo *El Xupet Negre*. Just across Avinguda del Paral·lel, in Poble Sec, artists can legally paint all over the concrete walls of the **Jardins de les Tres Xemeneies skate park** (Map p62, C6). Dive into it all on an artist-led tour with **Barcelona Street Style** (p28) or **Be Local** (www. belocaltours.com).

include the basement (with its mushroom-shaped brick pillars), the magnificent music room and the rooftop's fanciful mosaic-adorned chimney pots. (www. palauguell.cat)

Rambla del Raval   STREET

3 ⊙ MAP P62, B4

This broad boulevard was laid out in 2000 as part of the city's plan to open up the formerly

sleazy neighbourhood, with some success. Now with palm trees, terrace cafes and a weekend craft market, it is presided over by the glossy **Barceló Raval** (www.barcelo. com; ❄ 🛜) hotel and Fernando Botero's 7m-long, 2m-tall bronze sculpture of a plump cat, **El Gat de Botero**.

Antic Hospital de la Santa Creu   HISTORIC BUILDING

4 ⊙ MAP P62, C4

Behind the Mercat de La Boqueria stands what was once the city's main hospital. Founded in 1401, the Gothic Hospital of the Holy Cross functioned until the 1930s and was considered one of the best in Europe in its medieval heyday – it is famously the place where Antoni Gaudí died in 1926. Today it houses the **Biblioteca de Catalunya** (with its distinctive Gothic arches); the ceramic-covered **Institut d'Estudis Catalans** (www.iec.cat), accessible only by guided tour; and a soothing garden where people play chess. Its 15th-century former chapel, **La Capella** (http:// lacapella.barcelona), shows temporary exhibitions.

Centre de Cultura Contemporània de Barcelona   GALLERY

5 ⊙ MAP P62, B2

A dazzling complex of auditoriums, exhibition spaces and conference halls, the CCCB opened in 1994 in what was formerly an 18th-century hospice, the Casa de la Caritat. The courtyard, with a vast glass wall on one side, is spectacular. With 4500 sq metres of galleries, the centre hosts a constantly changing arts-and-culture programme. (CCCB; www.cccb.org)

Església de Sant Pau del Camp
CHURCH

6 MAP P62, B5

Barcelona's best example of Romanesque architecture is the dainty little cloister of this small church founded in the 9th or 10th century and later rebuilt in the 11th or 12th century. The cloister's 13th-century polylobulated arches are unique in Europe, sitting atop intricately carved capitals that depict scenes such as Adam and Eve with the serpent. The church itself contains the tombstone of Guifré II, son of Guifré el Pelós, a 9th-century count considered the founding father of Catalonia. (https://stpaudelcamp.blogspot.com)

Eating

Bar Central
CAFE €

7 MAP P62, B3

A fabulous tucked-away cafe-bar has taken over the palm-studded courtyard gardens and the priest's house of El Raval's 16th-century Casa de la Misericòrdia (a former orphanage). Speciality coffee, Catalan vermouths and all-natural wines accompany perfectly flaky croissants, tapas of tortilla and

delicate *entrepans* (filled rolls). Find it via **La Central bookshop** (www.lacentral.com;)

Cañete
TAPAS €€

8 MAP P62, D4

Epitomising Spain's smartened-up traditional tapas bars, always-busy Cañete centres on a bustling open kitchen with a marble-topped bar and an Andalucian patio at the back. The long list of uber-fresh, local-sourced tapas and *platillos* (sharing plates) packs in modern twists alongside classic favourites, including gooey tortillas, honey-drizzled aubergines, *boquerones* (anchovies) and *tortillitas de camarones* (shrimp fritters). (www.barcanete.com;)

El Pachuco
MEXICAN €

9 MAP P62, B5

Arrive early or jump on the wait list – this tiny, narrow and deservedly popular *mezcalería/taquería* gets completely packed with a low-key fashionable crowd. Exposed lightbulbs, dim lighting, bar stools and shelves cluttered with booze bottles and religious icons set the scene for irresistible tacos, quesadillas, guacamole and margaritas. There's a Barri Gòtic sister branch, La Pachuca (p52). (www.facebook.com/pachucobcn)

Suculent
CATALAN €€

10 MAP P62, C5

Part of celebrity chef Carles Abellán's culinary empire, this old-style bistro showcases the best of contemporary Catalan cuisine courtesy of El Bulli-trained Valencian chef Toni Romero. From red-prawn ceviche with avocado to black-butter ray and steak tartare over grilled bone marrow, only the finest market-fresh ingredients make it on to the smartly executed, tradition-rooted menu. (https://suculent.com; 📶)

Sésamo   VEGETARIAN €

11 ❌ MAP P62, A4

Regularly lauded as one of the city's best veggie restaurants, fun and cosy Sésamo transforms fresh, local ingredients into artful tapas with lashings of creativity – including figs stuffed with balsamic-drizzled feta and roast cabbage with mint pesto. Most people go for the seven-course tapas menu, and specials are chalked up on the board. (📶 ✏️)

Caravelle   INTERNATIONAL €

12 ❌ MAP P62, B3

Beloved of El Raval's stylish crowd, this soulful little cafe/restaurant serves creative international-style brunches that see queues snaking out the door, from halloumi-corn fritters and *huevos rancheros* to cauliflower shawarma and blow-out burgers. Coffee comes from Nømad (p89), while craft beers are home-brewed. (www.caravellebcn.com; 📶)

Bar Marsella (p69)

Bacaro

ITALIAN €€

13 MAP P62, C3

Widely considered one of Barcelona's top Italian restaurants, Bacaro delivers delicately crafted Venetian cuisine with contemporary flair in a slender alley setting just behind the Mercat de la Boqueria. It's a warm, low-key yet stylish split-level spot in which to tuck into beautiful seasonal plates of, perhaps, wild-mushroom *passatelli*, grilled-aubergine carpaccio or burrata drizzled with basil oil. (www.bacarobarcelona.com)

Veggie Garden

VEGAN €

14 MAP P62, B3

Sit amid bright murals while charming staff serve a ridiculously good-value South Asian-inspired menu of plant-based thalis, curries, salads, veggie burgers, pastas and tapas to a fun crowd, with all ingredients locally sourced. There's a three-course *menú del dia*, plus another branch nearby at Gran Via de les Corts Catalanes 602. (https://veggiegardengroup. com; 🖉)

Frankie Gallo Cha Cha Cha

PIZZA €€

15 MAP P62, C5

A cheeky, contemporary pizza joint every bit as cool as its Raval location, with a cavernous interior, natural wines, loud music and a lively vibe. Wood-fired pizzas range from traditional (cotto funghi) to creative (figs, burrata and

Festes de la Mercè

Held over four days around 24 September, in honour of one of Barcelona's two patron saints, the city's biggest party (www. barcelona.cat/merce) involves concerts, dancing and street theatre across town. There are also *castells* (human towers), fireworks synchronised with the Montjuïc fountains, *gegants* (papier-mâché giants), *sardanes* (Catalan dancing) and *correfocs* (fireworks-spitting demons).

porchetta) and involve artisanal Spanish and Italian ingredients. (https://frankiegallochachacha.com)

Flax & Kale

HEALTH FOOD €€

16 MAP P62, A2

Catalan chef Teresa Carles' self-styled 'healthy flexitarian restaurant' is a chic, sprawling, palm-dotted world where 80% of the menu is plant-based. Raw, vegan and gluten-free options abound; dishes wander from tuna bibimbap to grilled-aubergine ravioli to Panang red curry; and the leafy terrace has its own spice garden. (www.teresacarles. com; 🛜 🖉)

Ca L'Estevet

CATALAN €€

17 MAP P62, A3

On the Raval scene since 1890, this classic old-timer is known

Out & About in El Raval

The shadowy side streets of El Raval are dotted with scores of bars and clubs, and despite its vestigial edginess, this is a great place to go out. You'll find super-fashionable cocktail spots alongside great old taverns that have been the hangouts of the city's Bohemians since Picasso's time. The lower (southern) end of El Raval has a history of insalubriousness, particularly around Carrer de Sant Pau. Keep your wits about you.

for its traditional Catalan cooking, with uncomplicated recipes revolving around fresh market produce. Bright tiles, wine bottles and black-and-white photos of famous guests line the walls, while seasonal specialities include *escalivada* (smoky grilled vegetables), *cap i pota* (a tripe-like stew) and meat-stuffed *canelons* (Catalan-style cannelloni). (www. restaurantestevet.com)

Mirch INDIAN €

18 MAP P62, B3

A street-style contemporary Indian kitchen with European flair, Mirch is the colourful Raval brainchild of well-known chef Ivan Surinder. There are just a handful of sharing tables, where you can devour silky bowl-style curries (red-lentil

dahl, *palak paneer*) or the popular butter-chicken *vada pavs*, with a mango lassi on the side. (www. mirchbarcelona.com)

Drinking

Two Schmucks COCKTAIL BAR

19 MAP P62, A3

Originally a wandering pop-up bar, edgy yet unpretentious Two Schmucks has become one of Barcelona's (and Europe's) most talked-about cocktail bars, sweeping multiple awards and channelling a glammed-up dive-bar vibe. The team also runs brunchy restaurant **Fat Schmuck**. (www. facebook.com/schmuckordie)

La Confiteria BAR

20 MAP P62, B6

A vision of tiled floors, wood-covered walls and marble-topped tables, this evocative cocktail hang-out is a trip back to the 19th century – but with Bloody Marys and other craft liquid mixes. Until the 1980s it was a confectioner's shop, and the look barely changed with its conversion courtesy of one of Barcelona's foremost teams in nightlife wizardry. (www. confiteria.cat; 🛜)

Dalston Coffee COFFEE

21 🚇 MAP P62, B2

Inspired by East London's third-wave coffee scene, Dalston specialises in seasonal, traceable beans sourced from fincas around the world and roasted by barista Borja Roselló. Grab a velvety flat white to go, perhaps with a just-toasted *bikini* sandwich. (https://dalstoncoffee.com)

La Monroe

BAR

22 MAP P62, C4

At the Filmoteca de Catalunya's (p70) lively LGBTIQ+-friendly cafe-bar, floor-to-ceiling windows beam light across wooden tables, rickety chairs and a cobbled floor that mimics the square outside. Pop in for great cocktails, house vermouths, a good-value *menú del dia* and delectable tapas (Padrón peppers, ham croquettes). (www.lamonroe.es; 📶)

Caribbean Club

COCKTAIL BAR

23 MAP P62, C2

The dimly lit ship-like interior, with low wooden beams and cocktail shakers in glass cabinets, is just a taster at this elegant cocktail spot headed up by respected barman Juanjo González Rubiera, where Caribbean rums steal the show. It started life back in the 1970s as the sister bar to celebrated Boadas (p54). (www.caribbeanclubbcn.com; 📶)

Moog

CLUB

24 MAP P62, D5

Hosting both emerging and well-established DJ names, this fun and minuscule electronic club is

a standing favourite, with house, techno and electro in the main area, and indie/pop upstairs. (www.moogbarcelona.com)

Bar Marsella

BAR

25 MAP P62, C5

Going strong since 1820, with tiled floors and glinting chandeliers, Bar Marsella has served the likes of Dalí, Picasso, Gaudí and Hemingway, who was known to slump here over a potent *absenta* (absinthe), which is still the speciality.

Carrer de Joaquín Costa

With its mix of student vibes, contemporary-cocktail wizardry and old-school atmosphere, Carrer de Joaquín Costa is *the* place to hit the bars. Start with **Two Schmucks**, for some of Barcelona's most original cocktails. Other always-popular cocktail spots include **Negroni** (Map p62, A3; www.negronicocktailbar.com), the clue's in the name; **33 | 45** (Map p62, B4; https://3345.es; 📶), for mojitos, art, DJs; and **Lucky Schmuck** (Map p62, A3; https://schmuckordie.com) (whiskey-based cocktails). Old-timer **Casa Almirall** (p61) is a classic Modernista hang-out.

El Raval Drinking

Entertainment

Filmoteca de Catalunya

CINEMA

26 ⭐ MAP P62, C4

Relocated from Sarrià in 2012 as part of plans to revive El Raval's cultural offerings, Catalonia's national cinema occupies a modern 6000-sq-metre building amid the most louche part of the *barri*. It also comprises a film library, a bookshop and lively La Monroe cafe-bar (p69). (www.filmoteca.cat)

JazzSí Club

LIVE MUSIC

27 ⭐ MAP P62, A4

A cramped little bar run by the Taller de Músics (Musicians' Workshop) school and foundation, staging a varied programme of jazz jams, Cuban nights and flamenco. (http://tallerdemusics.com)

Shopping

Grey Street

HOMEWARES

28 🔒 MAP P62, B4

Named for the Canberra home of Australian owner Amy Cocker's grandparents, this stylishly reimagined former perfume shop is crammed with tempting trinkets, many of them crafted by local or Spanish artists – handpainted ceramic mugs and plant pots, fair-trade incense, tarot cards, patterned wall prints and essential oils. (www.greystreetbarcelona.com)

La Nostra Ciutat

ARTS & CRAFTS

29 🔒 MAP P62, B3

The creative work of Catalan artists fills this cheerful boutique, with a few branches around the city centre. Pick up snazzy Barcelona-map prints by Idmary Hernandez, prints of iconic Modernista buildings by Daniella Ferretti, tote bags depicting Gaudían tiles, jazzy Wouf laptop sleeves and beautiful stationery. (https://lanostraciutat.co)

Les Topettes

COSMETICS

30 🔒 MAP P62, A3

Globe-trotting products at this chic little temple to soap and perfume are handpicked by journalist Lucía and chef/interior designer Oriol. Gorgeously packaged scents, candles, soaps and creams from Diptyque, Cowshed, Hierbas de Ibiza, Antic Mallorca and more all have an environmental focus. (www.lestopettes.com)

Miscelánea

ART

31 🔒 MAP P62, B3

It's all about bold graphic design by emerging local and international artists at neighbourhood gallery Miscelánea's light-flooded shop, where wonderfully original prints mingle with indie mags and hand-painted ceramics. (https://miscelanea.info)

Vintage Boutiques

Some of Barcelona's most original vintage dens are hidden around El Raval, particularly along Carrer de la Riera Baixa and Carrer dels Tallers.

El Flea (Map p62, D6; https://fleamarketbcn.com) A lively monthly secondhand market packed with everything from vintage denim jackets to preloved novels.

Holala! Plaza (Map p62, B2; www.holala-ibiza.com) Inspired by Ibiza's long-established hippie-fashion scene, with bright pieces, lots of denim and recycled textiles sourced around the globe. Also on Carrer dels Tallers.

Flamingos Vintage Kilo (Map p62, D2; www.flamingosvintagekilo.com) With several Barcelona **outposts**, Flamingos deals in pay-by-weight American fashion from the 1940s to 1990s.

La Principal (Map p62, B3; https://laprincipalretro.com; Carrer d'Elisabets 3) Logo-stamped T-shirts, designer jeans, festival-vibe shirts and other vintage beauties.

Teranyina
ARTS & CRAFTS

32 MAP P62, B3

At artist Teresa Rosa Aguayo's textiles studio, in the heart of northern El Raval, you can join workshops at the loom, admire the beautiful pieces (silk scarves, botanical-themed shawls) and, of course, buy them. Natural dyes and fibres are key to the artisanal creation process. (www.textilteranyina.com)

Lantoki
FASHION & ACCESSORIES

33 MAP P62, B3

Designers Urko Martinez and Sandra Liberal handcraft their own minimalist women's fashion in this bright, breezy El Raval studio–boutique. The emphasis is on original, slow-fashion artisanal collections, and there are also design-your-own-clothes workshops. (www.lantoki.es)

Fantastik
ARTS & CRAFTS

34 MAP P62, A3

Over 500 products, such as woodland dolls, tin robots, ceramic bowls, vintage posters and rubber tablecloths, fill this colourful shop, which sources its collection from countries such as India, China, Morocco, Germany, Mexico and Japan. (www.fantastik.es)

Explore ⊕
La Ribera
& El Born

Originally medieval Barcelona's commercial epicentre, this charming and busy quarter hosts some of the city's liveliest tapas bars and most original boutiques, along with key sights such as the Museu Picasso, the Basílica de Santa Maria del Mar, the Palau de la Música Catalana and the leafy Parc de la Ciutadella. The bustling tangle of streets around the basilica is known as El Born.

The Short List

○ **Basílica de Santa Maria del Mar (p78)** *Admiring the beauty of Barcelona's finest example of Catalan Gothic, built with help from local parishioners.*

○ **Museu Picasso (p74)** *Discovering the origins of Picasso's genius at this fascinating museum spread across a series of medieval palaces.*

○ **Bar-hopping in El Born (p80)** *Tucking into tapas and sipping Catalan wines in El Born's buzz.*

○ **Palau de la Música Catalana (p84)** *Taking in a performance or exploring on a tour of this marvellous Modernista concert hall, then popping into the Mercat de Santa Caterina.*

○ **Parc de la Ciutadella (p84)** *Strolling, having a picnic, spotting the artworks or joining a yoga class.*

Getting There

Ⓜ Línia 4 stops at Urquinaona, Jaume I and Barceloneta. Línia 1 also stops nearby, at Urquinaona and Arc de Triomf (the nearest stop for Parc de la Ciutadella).

Neighbourhood Map on p82

Palau de la Música Catalana (p84) CCAT82/SHUTTERSTOCK ©

Top Experience 📷
Dive into the Museu Picasso's Art & Architecture

The setting alone, in five contiguous medieval stone mansions, makes Barcelona's Museu Picasso unique. While the collection concentrates on Málaga-born Pablo Picasso's formative years and early talent, there is also plenty of material from better-known periods to showcase the artist's versatility and genius. You come away feeling that Picasso was a true original, always one step ahead.

◉ MAP P82, E5

www.museupicasso.bcn.cat

History of the Museum

Allegedly it was Picasso himself who proposed the museum's creation in 1960, to his friend and personal secretary Jaume Sabartés, a Barcelona native. Three years later, the 'Sabartés Collection' was opened, since a museum bearing Picasso's name would have been met with censorship – Picasso's opposition to the Franco regime was well known. The Museu Picasso we see today opened in 1983. It originally held only Sabartés' personal collection of Picasso's art and a handful of other works, but the collection gradually expanded with donations from Salvador Dalí and Sebastià Junyer Vidal, among others. However, the largest part of the present collection came from Picasso himself. His widow, Jacqueline Roque, also donated 41 ceramic pieces and the *Woman with Bonnet* painting after Picasso's death.

Sabartés' contribution is honoured here with Picasso's famous Blue Period portrait of him wearing a ruff.

The Collection

The more than 3500 artworks are strongest on Picasso's earliest years, up until 1904, which is apt considering the artist spent his formative creative years in Barcelona. What makes this collection truly impressive – one-of-a-kind among the world's many Picasso museums – is the way in which it displays Picasso's extraordinary talent at such a young age. Masterpieces such as the enormous *Science and Charity* or *Portrait of Aunt Pepa*, as well as some self-portraits and the portraits of his parents, dating from 1896, shine a light on Picasso's precocious talent.

Early Days

The first two rooms hold sketches and oils from Picasso's early years in Málaga and A Coruña (1893–95), and lead on to his formative years in Barcelona. *Portrait of Aunt Pepa* (room 2), done in Málaga in 1896, shows the maturity of his

★ **Top Tips**

○ Avoid queues by booking tickets online and choosing a time slot (though it's almost always busy).

○ At €15, the Carnet del Museu Picasso annual pass is barely more expensive than an adult day pass (€12), and allows multiple entries.

○ Admission is free on Thursday evening and the first Sunday of the month.

○ Guided tours (€6) run on Sundays in Catalan, Spanish, English and French; there's an additional English tour on Tuesdays.

✗ **Take a Break**

Just a few doors north along Carrer de Montcada, Brunells 1852 (p87) is perfect for locally roasted coffee and some of Barcelona's best croissants.

Or wander up to Bar del Pla (p81) for traditional-with-a-twist tapas.

La Ribera & El Born Museu Picasso

brush strokes and his ability to portray character – at the tender age of 15. As you walk into room 3, you'll see the enormous *Science and Charity*, painted in 1897; faced with the technical virtuosity of such a painting, it seems almost inconceivable that it could have been created by the hands of a 15-year-old. His ingeniousness extends to his models too, with his father standing in for the doctor, and a beggar, whom he hired off the street along with her offspring, modelling the sick woman and the child. This painting caused the young artist to be noticed in the higher echelons of Spain's art world when *Science and Charity* was awarded an Honorary Mention at the General Fine Arts Exhibition in Madrid in 1897.

Also here is a series of rural landscapes from Picasso's time in Horta de Sant Joan in 1898 and early 1899.

Catalan Avant-Garde & Blue Period

Picasso returned to Barcelona in 1899 and joined what was known as the 'Catalan avant-garde', which you'll see in room 4. The scene revolved around the Barri Gòtic's Els Quatre Gats tavern (p52), where Picasso's first individual exhibition was held in 1900; it was also during this time that he delved into the human figure and developed his signature taste for landscapes seen from a window. In rooms 5 to 7 there are paintings from 1899–1901, along with a series of bullfighting sketches and *The Wait (Margot)*, a dramatically colourful Parisian piece from 1901, influenced by Van Gogh.

Room 8 is dedicated to the first significant new stage in Picasso's development, the Blue Period. *Woman with Bonnet* (1901) is an important work from this period, depicting a detainee from the Saint-Lazare women's prison and venereal disease hospital, which Picasso visited when in Paris – it also sets up the theme of Picasso's fascination with those inhabiting the down-and-out layers of society. The nocturnal blue-tinted views of *Roofs of Barcelona* (1903; room 8) and *The Madman* (often on loan) are cold and cheerless, yet somehow alive. *Roofs of Barcelona* is typical of the period, when Picasso frequently painted the city rooftops from different perspectives.

Early Cubism

Picasso did many drawings of beggars, the blind and the impoverished throughout 1903 and 1904. This leads to the 1905 painting of Benedetta Bianco, from Picasso's Pink Period (in room 9; also called *Retrato de la señora Canals*), and then to the beginnings of Cubism. Though the Museu Picasso is no showcase for his Cubist period, it does hold a few examples; check out the 1924 *Glass and Tobacco Packet* still-life painting (in room 11), a beautiful and simple work that marks the beginning of his fascination with still life.

Las Meninas Through the Prism of Picasso

From 1954 to 1962, Picasso was obsessed with the idea of researching and 'rediscovering' the greats, in particular Velázquez. In 1957 he made a series of renditions of Velázquez' masterpiece *Las meninas* (The Ladies-in-Waiting), now displayed in rooms 12 to 14. It is as though Picasso has looked at the original Velázquez painting through a prism reflecting all the styles he had worked through until then, creating his own masterpiece in the process. This is a wonderful opportunity to see *Las meninas* in its entirety, in a beautiful space, with stone arches framing some of the many canvases.

Across the hall, in room 15, you'll find *The Pigeons*, a series of nine canvases that Picasso painted on a break from his study of *Las meninas*, depicting the doves through his studio window in Cannes. Picasso's images of doves are inspired by the works of his father, José Ruiz Blasco, with whom he created his first sketches.

Ceramics

What is also special about the Museu Picasso is its showcasing of his work in lesser-known media. Rooms B1, B2 and N contain Picasso's engravings and 42 ceramic pieces completed throughout the latter years of his unceasingly creative life. You'll see plates and bowls decorated with simple, single-line drawings of fish, owls and other animal shapes, typical for Picasso's daubing on clay. Enjoy *Bullfighting Scene with Fish*, done on a glazed Spanish plate.

Llotja de Mar

Around five minutes' walk south of the Museu Picasso, Barcelona's

Getting Around the Collection

The permanent collection is housed in the Palau Aguilar, Palau del Baró de Castellet and Palau Meca, all dating to the 14th century. The 18th-century Casa Mauri, built over medieval remains (even some Roman leftovers have been identified), and the adjacent 14th-century Palau Finestres, accommodate temporary exhibitions. The elegant courtyards, galleries and staircases preserved in the first three buildings are as delightful as the collection inside.

medieval Stock Exchange, the **Llotja de Mar** (www.llotjademar. cat), was originally built in the 14th century. Though later extended with a neoclassical facade, it still retains much of its Gothic interior. In 1775, it went on to house the Reial Acadèmia (until 1970), where Picasso's father taught and the young artist studied before moving to Paris. There are guided tours on weekends (book ahead).

Homenatge a Picasso

On the west side of Parc de la Ciutadella, within a 10-minute stroll of the Museu Picasso, this typically impenetrable 1983 **piece by Antoni Tàpies** (Passeig de Picasso) sits near where Picasso's family once lived. Old furniture, steel girders and pieces of sheets and ropes sit within a glass box with water trickling down its panes, surrounded by a pool of water.

Top Experience 📷

Savour History at the Basílica de Santa Maria del Mar

At the southwestern end of Passeig del Born stands Barcelona's finest Catalan Gothic church, Santa Maria del Mar (Our Lady of the Sea). Begun in 1329, under the watch of architects Berenguer de Montagut and Ramon Despuig, the church is remarkable for its harmony and simplicity. It was funded by wealthy neighbourhood families and the parishioners helped construct the church.

◉ MAP P82, E6

www.santamariadel
marbarcelona.org

👫

Main Sanctuary

The pleasing unity of form and symmetry of the central nave and two flanking aisles owe much to the rapidity with which the church was built – a mere, record-breaking 53 years, on the site of the Romanesque Santa Maria de les Arenes church. The slender octagonal pillars create an enormous sense of lateral space, bathed in the light of stained glass. The walls, side chapels and facades were finished by 1350 and the entire structure was completed in 1383.

Ceiling & Side Chapels

Even before anarchists gutted the church in 1909 and again in 1936 (when it famously burned for 11 days straight), Santa Maria always lacked superfluous decoration. Gone are the gilded chapels that weigh heavily on so many Spanish churches, while the splashes of colour high above the nave are subtle – unusually and beautifully so. It all serves to highlight the church's fine proportions, purity of line and sense of space.

The Porters

It's often said that the city's *bastaixos* (porters) spent a day each week carrying the stone required to build the church from royal quarries in Montjuïc, but in fact the stone arrived by boat. The porters' memory lives on in reliefs of them in the main doors and stone carvings elsewhere in the church – a reminder that Santa Maria was conceived as a people's church.

Tickets & Tours

From 10am to 6pm Monday to Saturday and 1.30pm to 5pm on Sunday, visitors must pay to enter the church (€5). A €10 ticket adds on a trip up to the towers and rooftop. If timings coincide (check online), it's well worth joining an expert-led tour.

★ **Top Tips**

○ Don't miss the urban views from the rooftop.

○ If your purpose is spiritual, there is a daily mass at 7.30pm.

○ Enquire in the gift shop as to whether any baroque music recitals are scheduled for the evening.

✕ **Take a Break**

Admire the western facade of the church while enjoying tapas and Catalan wines at one of the outdoor tables of La Vinya del Senyor (p81) or over vermouth and cider at El Chigre 1769 (p88).

Alternatively, pop around to Euskal Etxea (p81) for a feast of Basque *pintxos* (tapas).

Walking Tour

Tapas & Bar-Hopping in El Born

El Born, the tangle of medieval-origin streets surrounding the Basílica de Santa Maria del Mar and Passeig del Born, snapshots all that's irresistible about Barcelona. Join the throng for fabulous tapas, hidden-away wine bars, lively vermouth stops and more after-dark fun.

Walk Facts

Start Bar del Pla; Ⓜ Jaume I

End Bormuth; Ⓜ Barceloneta, Ⓜ Jaume I

Distance 1km; three to four hours

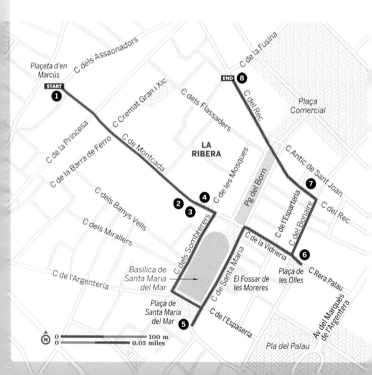

❶ Bar del Pla

An energetic long-time favourite, with Catalan tiling and vaulted ceilings, Bar del Pla (www.bardelpla.cat; 📶) does creative Catalan-rooted tapas such as ham croquettes, wasabi mushrooms and rice of the day.

❷ El Xampanyet

Wander down Carrer de Montcada to El Xampanyet (www.elxampanyet.es; 📶), one of Barcelona's best-known *cava* (sparkling wine) bars; pack in for homemade tapas, including tortillas and *boquerones* (anchovies).

❸ Bodega La Puntual

At lively traditional-feel La Puntual (https://grupovarela.es), with wine-barrel tables and wheels of cheese at the door, *cava* and homemade vermouth pair with fuss-free tapas (Spanish cheeses, ham croquettes).

❹ Euskal Etxea

Next up: the drool-worthy *pintxos* at stone-walled Euskal Etxea (www.gruposagardi.com; 📶) – from prawns topped with peppers to deep-fried goat's cheese.

❺ La Vinya del Senyor

Relax on the terrace opposite the basilica or crowd into the tiny bottle-lined bar at La Vinya del Senyor (www.facebook.com/vinyadelsenyor; 📶). World-wandering wines, cheese platters and cold meats keep you going.

❻ Cal Pep

Most people are happy elbowing their way to the bar for some of the tastiest seafood tapas in town, such as *cloïsses amb pernil* (clams and ham), at legendary, boisterous Cal Pep (www.calpep.com).

❼ Farola

From soulful jazz to foot-stomping flamenco, live music meets expertly crafted cocktails and carefully curated sherries at lively Farola (www.farolabcn.com).

❽ Bormuth

With a perfect terrace, Bormuth (https://bormuthbarcelona.com; 📶) specialises in homemade vermouth on tap, but also serves *cava*, artisan beers, Catalan wines and wonderful tapas (tortilla, Padrón peppers).

La Ribera & El Born

Ronda de Sant Pere

A **B** **C** **D**

1

C del Bruc

C de Trafalgar

C de Méndez Núñez

C de Lluís
el Piadós

31

10

Plaça de
Sant Pere

C del Rec Comtal

C d'en Cortines

Passatge
de Sert

Ptge de Sert

C de Trafalgar

Róuri
Ici et Là

Ptge de les
Manufactures

23

9

Formatgeria
Simó

C de les Basses
de Sant Pere

2

C d'Ortigosa

C d'en Monec

C d'en Llàstics

C dels Metges

Plaça del
Pou de la
Figuera

C de Sant Pere més Alt

C de Sant Pere Mitjà

C de Sant Pere més Baix

LA RIBERA

C de Jaume Giralt

17

18

Palau de
la Música
Catalana

1

27

C de Mare de Déu del Pilar

C de Verdaguer i Callís

C del Fonollar

3

C Palau de
la Música

C d'en Giralt i Pellisser

C dels Carders

Via Laietana

C dels Mercaders

Av de Francesc Cambó

2
Mercat
de Santa
Caterina

13

C de
Colomines

Capella d'en
Marcús

34

4

C del Dr Joaquim Pou

C de les Freixures

Colmillo
de Morsa

C dels Carders

1

C de
Montcada

Plaça
d'Antoni
Maura

C dels Mercaders

5

Av de la Catedral

C de la Borra

C de la Princesa

8

C Vigatans

Colmado

For reviews see

	Top Experiences	p74
	Sights	p84
	Eating	p86
	Drinking	p88
	Shopping	p91

Plaça de Ramon
Berenguer
el Gran

Plaça de
l'Àngel

C del Sots-Tinent Navarro

Jaume I

Via Laietana

C del
Brosoli

C de l'Argenter

C de
Manresa

6

N 0 _____ 200 m
0 _____ 0.1 miles

A **B** **C** **D**

E
F
G
H

1

2

3

4

5

6

La Ribera & El Born

Plaça del Comerç

Pg de Lluís Companys

C del Portal Nou

Pg de Lluís Companys

Pg de Pujades

C del Comerç

Parc de la Ciutadella
3

Museu de Zoologia
(Castell dels
Tres Dragons)

L'Hivernacle
(Arboretum)

Museu de
Geologia

L'Umbracle
(Arboretum)

C d'en Tantarantana

C d'Allada Vermell

C de la Princesa

Pg de Picasso

C de la Fusina

C Comercial

C dels Assaonadors

C dels Flassaders

Born Centre de
Cultura i Memòria

Plaça
Comercial

C de la Ribera

Museu
Picasso

Moco
Museum

25
26

11

7
5

Museu de
Cultures
del Món

EL BORN

33

Passeig
del Born

4

C Antic de Sant Joan

C del Comerç

Av del Marquès de l'Argentera

24

C de Montcada

C de l'Esparteria

C del Bonaire

C del Rec

Estació
de França

32

C dels Sombrerers

19

C de la Vidrieria

C de
Santa Maria

28

C Rera Palau

C d'Ocata

16

Basílica de
Santa Maria
del Mar

21

30

Plaça de
Santa Maria
del Mar

29

E
F
G
H

12

15

20

6

1

Sights

Palau de la Música Catalana
ARCHITECTURE

1 ◉ MAP P82, A3

A fantastical symphony in tile, brick, sculpted stone and stained glass, this Unesco-listed, 2146-seat concert hall is a high point of Barcelona's Modernista architecture. Built for the Orfeó Català musical society between 1905 and 1908 by Domènech i Montaner, with the help of some of the best Catalan artisans of the time, it was conceived as a temple for the Catalan Renaixença (Renaissance). The showstopper is the richly colourful auditorium, with its ceiling of blue-and-gold stained glass and a shimmering 1000kg skylight. Shows are highly recommended; you can also visit for a 50-minute tour (guided or self-guided). (www.palaumusica.cat)

Mercat de Santa Caterina
MARKET

2 ◉ MAP P82, C4

Come shopping for your tomatoes or pop in for lunch at Bar Joan (p87) at this extraordinary-looking produce market, designed by forward-thinking architects Enric Miralles and Benedetta Tagliabue to replace its 19th-century predecessor. Completed in 2005 (sadly after Miralles' death in 2000), it stands out for its undulating, kaleidoscopic ceramic roof, which recalls the Modernista tradition of *trencadís* (mosaic) decoration. Inside, bustling stalls, restaurants, cafes and bars huddle between twisting slender branches resembling grey steel trees. (www.mercatsantacaterina.com)

Parc de la Ciutadella
PARK

3 ◉ MAP P82, H2

People flock to the city's most central green lung for a stroll, a picnic, a boat ride on the lake, a yoga class or a prebooked tour of Catalonia's **parliament** (www.parlament.cat), and to marvel at the swirling 19th-century **waterfall-fountain** in which Gaudí had a hand. After the War of the Spanish Succession, Felipe V razed a swath of La Ribera to build the Ciutadella fortress, designed to keep watch over Barcelona. Only in 1869 did the central government allow its demolition; the site was turned into a park and adapted for Barcelona's 1888 Universal Exposition by Josep Fontserè, with Josep Vilaseca's Mudéjar-style **Arc de Triomf** added in 1888. (👫)

Passeig del Born
STREET

4 ◉ MAP P82, F5

Framed at each end by the majestic Basílica de Santa Maria del Mar (p78) and the former Mercat del Born, leafy Passeig del Born was Barcelona's main playground from the 13th to 18th century. It's here in this graceful setting beneath the trees that El Born's essential appeal shines – thronging people, brilliant bars and restaurants, and architecture from a medieval film set.

Moco Museum
MUSEUM

5 MAP P82, E5

El Born's 16th-century Palau dels Cervelló has been reimagined as a dazzling creative space devoted to contemporary, modern and street art, courtesy of Amsterdam's independent Moco Museum, which opened its second branch in Barcelona in late 2021. Thought-provoking pieces by Kusama, Banksy, Warhol, Basquiat, Dalí and more feature among the carefully curated collection, dramatically set against red-brick arches and mirrored walls. The immersive digital experience is a highlight. (https://mocomuseum.com)

Born Centre de Cultura i Memòria
HISTORIC BUILDING

6 MAP P82, G4

Originally launched for the tercentenary of the Catalan defeat in the War of the Spanish Succession (in 1714), this cultural space is housed in the former 19th-century Mercat del Born, designed by Catalan architect Josep Fontserè. Excavations in 2001 unearthed remains of whole streets (now exposed on the subterranean level), flattened to make way for the much-hated Ciutadella (citadel), along with necropolises from Roman and Islamic times. The building is free to access, or join a 90-minute guided tour among the ruins. (http://elbornculturaimemoria.barcelona.cat)

Parc de la Ciutadella

Carrer de Montcada

Running between the Romanesque **Capella d'en Marcús** (Map p82, D4), one of the city's oldest churches, and **Passeig del Born** (p84), this medieval high street was driven towards the sea from the road that, in the 12th century, led northeast from the city walls. It became Barcelona's most coveted address for the merchant classes, in what was the commercial heartland of medieval Barcelona. The great mansions that remain today mostly date from the 14th and 15th centuries.

Museu de Cultures del Món
MUSEUM

7 MAP P82, E5

The central-Barcelona outpost of Montjuïc's Museu Etnològic (p169) opens through a grand courtyard overlooked by an 18th-century staircase within the restored medieval Palau Nadal and Palau Marquès de Lió. Over 500 artefacts travel through the ancient cultures of Africa, Asia, the Americas and Oceania, with displays ranging from Andean weaving to Ethiopian religious art. (http://museuculturesmon.bcn.cat)

Eating

Can Cisa/ Bar Brutal
SPANISH €€

8 MAP P82, D5

Can Cisa's elegant all-natural wines pair beautifully with Bar Brutal's innovative reimagining of fresh Catalan ingredients at this rowdy, fashionable wine bar and restaurant from Barcelona culinary kings the Colombo brothers (and team). Straight from the open kitchen, creations such as tuna tartare, watermelon salad and delicate artisan cheeses pull in a fun crowd until late. (www.cancisa.cat)

Casa Lolea
TAPAS €

9 MAP P82, B2

Dangling strings of tomatoes and garlic, red-and-black-spot decor and white-brick walls lend an air of Andalucian charm to this stylish tapas-and-vermouth bar. It's popular for its lightly creative breakfast *entrepans* (filled rolls) and classic-with-a-twist tapas like garlic-and-mushroom scrambles, just-cooked tortilla, northern Spanish cheeses and Extremadura ham. (www.casalolea.com; 🛜)

Fismuler
MEDITERRANEAN €€€

10 MAP P82, D1

The brainchild of three ex El Bulli chefs, the minimalist Barcelona outpost of this Madrid-born market-based sensation is one of the city's hottest tickets. Daily-changing menus throw seasonal local produce into expertly executed, unpretentious dishes: artichoke-and-snail rice, Delta de l'Ebre oysters or grilled corvina with kimchi, followed by famously gooey cheesecake. (www.fismuler. com; 🖉)

Koku Kitchen   ASIAN €

11 ✖ MAP P82, G5

A stylish brick-walled space with scattered plants and communal tables, Koku serves delectable homemade bao stuffed with beef, pork, tofu or onion bhajis, sourcing most ingredients locally and hand-making its own noodles and gyoza daily. Some of Barcelona's best steaming ramen bowls emerge from the kitchen here, including vegetarian-friendly shiitake-broth options. Also in the Barri Gòtic (p52). (www.kokukitchen.es; 🛜🖉)

Picnic   CAFE €€

12 ✖ MAP P82, E2

Terrazzo-style tables, turquoise-tiled walls and scattered greenery set the buzzing scene at easy-going, Californian–Chilean-owned Picnic, one of Barcelona's brunch originals. The flavours of its owners' homelands are thoughtfully combined in berry-topped brioche French toast, punchy *huevos rancheros*, Mexican-feel *chilaquiles* and halloumi-and-aubergine tacos. (www.picnic-restaurant.com; 🛜🖉)

Bar Joan   CATALAN €

13 ✖ MAP P82, C4

A locally popular stop inside the Mercat de Santa Caterina (p84), with tall stools at the counter and a separate dining room, old-school Bar Joan is known especially for its *arròs negre* (cuttlefish-ink rice) on Tuesdays and paella on Thursdays. It's a simple, friendly and good-value spot for home-cooked tapas or the excellent-value *menú del dia*. (🛜)

Brunells 1852   CAFE €

14 ✖ MAP P82, D5

With coffee by locally loved El Magnífico (p91), divine pastries by Pastisseria Canal (known for its prize-winning flavoured croissants) and classic Barcelona recipes on the menu, this turquoise-styled cafe and bakery is a local hit. There's been a bakery here since 1852. (www.brunells.barcelona)

Tantarantana   MEDITERRANEAN €

15 ✖ MAP P82, E4

All patterned tiled floors, marble-top tables and wooden beams, shoebox-sized Tantarantana attracts a lively crowd. Market-driven Mediterranean tapas and small plates are prepared using local small-scale ingredients, from citrusy deep-fried aubergines to *ous estrellats* (fried eggs) with *ibérico* ham. The long bodega-like space has terrace tables at both ends. (www.gruposantelmo.com; 🛜)

El Chigre 1769

TAPAS €€

16 🌂 MAP P82, E6

Part Asturian cider house and part Catalan *vermuteria* (vermouth bar), this Slow Food-accredited hang-out brings elegant organic-fired versions of classic dishes from both regions to a stylishly revamped 18th-century building. The menu, devised by Asturian chef Fran Heras, features potatoes with Cabrales sauce, Picos de Europa cheeses, Asturian *fabada* and cured meats from the Pyrenees. (http://elchigre1769.com)

Mosquito

ASIAN €

17 🌂 MAP P82, D3

This pint-sized, always-busy, unadorned spot in El Born is devoted to great-value 'Asian tapas'. Local Catalan ingredients are worked into fragrant Vietnamese pho, salted edamame, Chinese dim sum and Japanese gyoza. The same switched-on team runs nearby Red Ant (noodles) and Grasshopper (ramen). (www.mosquitotapas.com)

Espai Mescladís

MEDITERRANEAN €

18 🌂 MAP P82, D3

Rainbow-coloured chairs and tables sit under medieval stone arches at this nonprofit social-project cafe-bar, which helps integrate immigrants to Barcelona. The North African–Mediterranean menu swings from hummus, tabbouleh and tagines to *patates braves* and fresh lemonade. Proceeds help fund cooking courses for people on the fringes of society. Also at La Ribera's **Sant Lluc art centre** (www.mescladis.org). (www.facebook.com/mescladis; 🌂)

Funky Bakers

DELI €

19 🌂 MAP P82, F6

Organic Km0 (local) ingredients and small local producers fuel the tempting spread at this takeout favourite. Grab an expertly poured coffee (with beans from Barcelona roaster Nømad) and a stuffed challah-bun breakfast sandwich to enjoy under the trees. Also runs L'Eixample's Funky Bakers Eatery (p126). (https://funkybakers.com)

Bar Celta

GALICIAN €

20 🌂 MAP P82, F4

The newer El Born branch of a beloved Barri Gòtic classic (p52), delightfully old-school Bar Celta showcases Galician cuisine in all its simple, fresh beauty. The signature tapa is *pop a feria* (Galician-style boiled octopus), or you might try salt-dusted Padrón peppers, grilled prawns, fresh *berberechos* (cockles) and wedges of home-cooked tortilla. (www.barcelta.com)

Drinking

Paradiso

COCKTAIL BAR

21 🍸 MAP P82, G6

Fabulous Paradiso is fronted by a snow-white, wardrobe-sized pastrami shop. But this is only the portal – step through the fridge to a glam speakeasy where highly creative, artfully prepared cocktails steal the show, beneath a tropical-garden ceiling. No surprise then that it won first spot on the World's 50 Best Bars list in 2022. (www.paradiso.cat; 🛜)

Dr Stravinsky
COCKTAIL BAR

22 🚇 MAP P82, E6

At this alchemist-inspired temple to crafted-cocktail wizardry, knockout signature drinks are mixed using house-made gin, its own essential oils and other home-grown ingredients. Behind chilli-red doors, the centuries-old building has been reborn in lab-like, vintage-loving style, with herb jars and flasks on the walls. (www.drstravinsky.cat)

Nømad Cøffee Lab & Shop
COFFEE

23 🚇 MAP P82, B2

Leader of Barcelona's third-wave coffee scene, Nømad is known for its seasonally sourced, small-batch, Barcelona-roasted beans and experimental techniques. Owner and barista Jordi Mestre was inspired by his time in London, and at this snug, lab-style cafe it's all about coffee tastings and expertly poured espresso, flat whites and cold brews. Also in Poblenou at Frutas Selectas (p105). (www.nomadcoffee.es)

Passatge de Sert

Just off Carrer de Sant Pere més Alt, this leafy 19th-century *passatge* (Map p82, B2) was once the textiles factory of the wealthy Sert family. Now refreshed, it's home to French-owned design shop **Ici et Là** (Map p82, B2; https://icietla.com) and Barcelona-made slow-fashion label **Róuri** (Map p82, B2; www.rouri-official.com), as well as coffee fave **Nømad** and tapas spot **Casa Lolea** (p86). Opposite, **Formatgeria Simó** (Map p82, B2) is a wonderland of European cheeses.

Creps al Born
COCKTAIL BAR

A rowdy, jam-packed and seriously fun party-loving cocktail bar, next door to Funky Bakers (see 19 🍴 MAP P82, F6), where people spill out onto Passeig del Born over wildly creative cocktails. Good crepes, too. Sister cocktail spot **Bar Sauvage** is another favourite. (www.facebook.com/CrepsalBorn)

Clubhaus
BAR

24 🚇 MAP P82, G5

Upstairs: graffiti-clad concrete walls, lively pool table, Mexican-style street food. Downstairs: table tennis, crafted cocktails, meaty American-inspired snacks, DJs later on. Multi-concept venture Clubhaus keeps up the pace from coffee to brunch to espresso martinis to late-night karaoke. (www.clubhaus.es)

El Diset

WINE BAR

25 MAP P82, F5

Dealing almost exclusively in Catalan drops, El Disset is a sleek, candlelit wine, cocktail and tapas bar that also does tastings. Thin *torrades* (toasted bread with toppings) and platters of Catalan cheeses and Iberian ham accompany glasses of Terra Alta,

El Born's Boutiques

Many of El Born's independent cutting-edge boutiques champion a slow-fashion ethos and celebrate local Barcelona brands. **Ozz Barcelona** (Map p82, E6; www.ozzstore.com; Carrer dels Banys Vells 8) is a particularly loved showcase of emerging urban designers; its neighbours **Angle** (Map p82, E6; https://anglestore.com; Carrer dels Mirallers 10), **Ivori** (Map p82, E6; www.ivoribarcelona.com; Carrer dels Mirallers 7) and **Colmado** (Map p82, D6; https://colmadoshop.com) all have fabulously original collections rooted in sustainable materials. Another favourite is Nordic-inspired **Colmillo de Morsa** (Map p82, D4; www.colmillodemorsa.com), by Elisabet Vallecillo and Javier Blanco.

Montsant, Penedès, Priorat and more. (https://eldiset.com)

Guzzo

COCKTAIL BAR

26 MAP P82, G5

With superb seasonal cocktails, regular live bands and good vibes anytime of day, this old-school cocktail bar is run by much-loved Barcelona DJ Fred Guzzo, who is often at the decks. The tempting Mediterranean-international tapas spread makes the most of fresh ingredients, from courgette-flower tempura to artisanal cheeses from nearby Vila Viniteca. On weekends there's live music. (www.guzzorestaurante.es;)

Antic Teatre

BAR

27 MAP P82, A3

There's often a queue for tables on the buzzy garden terrace at this relaxed community cafe-bar, hidden away in a 17th-century building, where proceeds go towards the Antic Teatre's cultural projects. (www.anticteatre.com;)

Mariposa Negra

COCKTAIL BAR

28 MAP P82, F6

With a terrace opening on to El Born's lively Plaça de les Olles, Mariposa Negra crafts wonderfully original cocktails using fresh ingredients like homemade limoncello, just-squeezed orange juice and the team's own vermouth. The eye-catching ceramic cups are made with 3D-printing technology. (https://mariposanegrabar.com)

Shopping

Vila Viniteca
WINE

29 🔒 MAP P82, F6

One of Barcelona's top wine stores, Vila Viniteca has been hunting down the finest local and imported wines since 1932. There are regular events, on-request tastings and a handful of bar tables, and on several November evenings cellars from across Spain present their young new wines. At No 9, **La Teca** shop is devoted to gourmet food products. (www.vilaviniteca.es)

El Magnífico
COFFEE

30 🔒 MAP P82, E6

All sorts of coffee beans, sourced seasonally from around the world, have been roasted at much-loved third-generation El Magnífico since the early 20th century. Grab a coffee to go. The family team also runs tea temple **Sans i Sans** (www.sansisans.com), opposite. (www.cafeselmagnifico.com)

Working in the Redwoods
CERAMICS

31 🔒 MAP P82, C1

Catalan designer Miriam Cernuda handcrafts beautiful, minimalist, earthy-toned bowls, mugs, vases, plates and other ceramics from all-natural materials, inspired by the colours of the Costa Brava (where she grew up). There are also occasional ceramics classes. (www.workingintheredwoods.com)

Casa Gispert
FOOD

32 🔒 MAP P82, E6

Behind a forest-green wooden shopfront, atmospheric Casa Gispert has been toasting nuts and selling all manner of dried fruit since 1851. Spiced chocolate, Spanish olive oils, La Mancha saffron and own-brand vermouth are among its other delights. (www.casagispert.com)

Hofmann Pastisseria
FOOD

33 🔒 MAP P82, F5

All painted wooden cabinets and Tiffany-blue interiors, this bite-sized gourmet patisserie is linked to Barcelona's prestigious Hofmann cooking school and was named Catalonia's best bakery in 2022. Don't miss the prize-winning mascarpone-filled croissants. (https://hofmann-bcn.com)

Mostaza
ARTS & CRAFTS

34 🔒 MAP P82, D4

A charming collection of hand-crafted pieces by Catalan and other Spanish creatives – fun animal-inspired ceramics, floral-themed watercolours, vegan candles, ceramic-based earrings and botanical-print notebooks. (https://mostazabcn.com)

Explore ◉
Barceloneta, the Waterfront & El Poblenou

Barcelona's formerly industrial waterfront now boasts sparkling beaches, ultramodern high-rises, yacht-filled marinas and a seaside promenade. The gateway to the Mediterranean is the old-fashioned fishing quarter of Barceloneta. To the northeast, post-industrial El Poblenou offers a raft of creative design spaces and a string of popular beaches stretching to modern El Fòrum.

The Short List

○ **El Poblenou Platges (p94)** *Basking on these sun-kissed sandy beaches, before a seafood lunch.*

○ **Barceloneta dining (p96)** *Sampling tapas at La Cova Fumada or Jai-Ca, or finding perfect paella.*

○ **Design in El Poblenou (p102)** *Wandering between third-wave cafes, lively street art and ambitious creative projects, such as Espacio 88.*

○ **Work up a sweat (p103)** *Enjoying sunrise paddle-boarding or a yoga class on the beach.*

○ **Museu Marítim (p100)** *Exploring this fascinating Gothic shipyard and Barcelona's rich maritime past.*

Getting There & Around

Ⓜ Drassanes, Barceloneta, Ciutadella Vila Olímpica, Llacuna, Bogatell, El Poblenou and El Maresme Fòrum are the best stops.

🚡 The Teleféric del Port runs to/from Montjuïc.

Neighbourhood Map on p98

L'Estel Ferit, by Rebecca Horn (p101) S74/SHUTTERSTOCK ©

Top Experience 📷

Soak up the Scene on El Poblenou's Beaches

A series of beautiful beaches dotted with sea-food restaurants and xiringuitos (beach bars) stretches northeast from the Port Olímpic to El Fòrum. Though El Poblenou Platges are largely artificial, sunseekers descend here in summer – and it's quieter than on the strands closer to the city centre. At other times of year, this is a popular spot for running, cycling and lunching.

◎ MAP P98, F3

Nova Icària & Bogatell

The southernmost and busiest of El Poblenou's beaches, with views of the Port Olímpic, broad, golden Platja de la Nova Icària gets lively in warmer months, when a couple of *xiringuitos* grace the sand and people gather on the beach-volleyball courts. Heading northwest, next up is buzzy Platja del Bogatell (pictured), fronting El Poblenou and boasting sunbeds, umbrellas and more volleyball. Several excellent year-round restaurants dot the promenade just above Bogatell, keeping things pleasantly lively, even in winter.

Mar Bella & Llevant

Next along, Platja de la Mar Bella has a small nudist strip and some water sports and is popular with the LGBTIQ+ crowd. Locally loved Platja de la Nova Mar Bella also has a bit of a watersports scene, and leads into the new Front Marítim residential and commercial waterfront strip. This is part of the Diagonal Mar project in the Fòrum district, which is fronted by the last and easternmost of these artificial beaches to be created, Platja del Llevant, completed in 2006 and popular with dog walkers.

El Fòrum

At the north end of the Parc del Fòrum, just east of the futuristic Edifici Fòrum, the **Zona de Banys** is a tranquil seawater swimming area won from the sea by the creation of massive cement-block barriers. There are kayaks, bikes and other activities to keep you busy, while cyclists, skateboarders and rollerbladers zip past. Just behind, an enormous photovoltaic panel turns its face up to the sun to power the area with solar energy.

★ **Top Tips**

• The main swimming season is from May to mid-September, when water temperatures can reach 24°C.

• These beaches offer plenty of activities: **Platja del Bogatell** has football and volleyball on the sand, while **Platja de la Mar Bella** has a skateboard area with half-pipes and is home to the **Base Nàutica Municipal** (www.basenautica. org), which organises kayaking and paddle-boarding trips and rents water-sports equipment.

✗ **Take a Break**

Overlooking Bogatell beach, Xiringuito Escribà (p102) is one of Barcelona's most popular seafood and rice restaurants. Next-door Can Fisher (p102) is also a delight.

Or pop just inland to the Rambla del Poblenou (p101) for coffee and tapas under the trees.

Walking Tour 🚶

Sea & Seafood in Barceloneta

Barcelona's Mediterranean roots are nowhere more pronounced than in sunny Barceloneta, a seaside peninsula with a salty air and an enduring relationship with the sea, which is on show with its ceramic wall tiles, maritime street names and neighbourhood festivals. Savour time-worn taverns, stylish cocktails bars and market buzz on this roam around the city's soulful seafaring barri.

Walk Facts

Start Can Paixano; Ⓜ Barceloneta

End Platja de la Barceloneta; Ⓜ Barceloneta

Length 1.6km; two hours, or as long as you like!

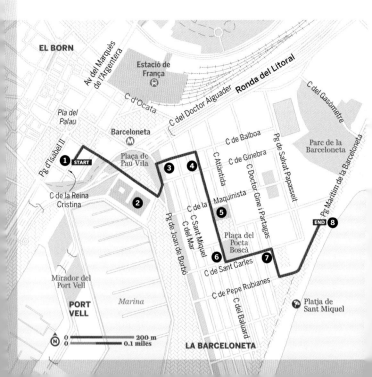

❶ Can Paixano

It doesn't come any more authentic than Can Paixano (La Xampanyeria; www.canpaixano.com), one of Barcelona's best old-style *cava* (sparkling wine) bars, founded in 1969. It's loved for its bubbly rosé, combined with bite-sized *entrepans* (filled rolls) and tapas.

❷ 1881

Head to the top floor of the Museu d'Història de Catalunya where you'll find elegant terrace bar-restaurant 1881 (www.gruposagardi.com; 📷), with a fabulous cocktail lounge overlooking the port and fresh seafood from Barceloneta's docks.

❸ Vaso de Oro

Always packed, old-school Vaso de Oro (www.vasodeoro.com) gathers a high-spirited crowd for fantastic tapas: grilled *gambes* (prawns), *patates amanides* (Andalucian-style potato salad) and *solomillo* (sirloin) chunks.

❹ Jai-Ca

In business since 1955 (and now with a second branch next-door), much-loved Jai-Ca (www.barjaica.com) serves up juicy grilled prawns, flavour-rich anchovies and tender octopus, with cold draught beer and crisp, bubbly *cava*.

❺ Mercat de la Barceloneta

Originally designed in 1884 by Antoni Rovira i Trias, Barceloneta's restored market (www.mercatdelabarceloneta.com) has seasonal produce, seafood stalls and sit-down restaurants, including traditional El Bar de Paco. Don't miss fourth-generation **Baluard Barceloneta** opposite, one of the city's best bakeries.

❻ La Cova Fumada

Tiny, frills-free, family-run La Cova Fumada (www.lacovafumada.com) is a Barceloneta (and Barcelona) legend. The secret? Mouth-watering octopus, calamari, sardines, grilled *carxofes* (artichokes) and signature *bombes* (meat-and-potato croquettes) – said to have been originally created right here.

❼ Bar Leo

An almost entirely *barcelonin* crowd spills out into the street from Bar Leo, a hole-in-the-wall drinking den plastered with images of late Andalucian singer Bambino (an acquaintance of the Granada-born owner).

❽ Platja de Barceloneta

Golden Platja de la Barceloneta, the beach closest to Barceloneta, is an iconic spot, though it gets busy with tourists and pickpocketing is common. It's best to visit first thing or for a sunset stroll, perhaps continuing northeast to the **Port Olímpic**.

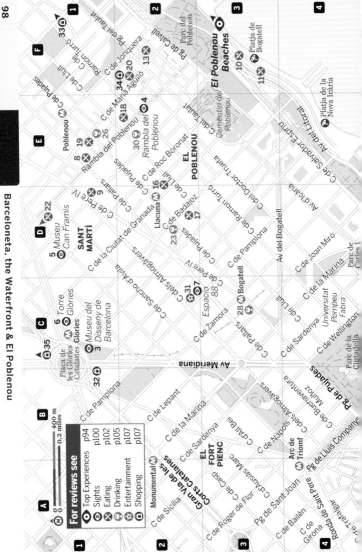

For reviews see

⊙	Top Experiences	p94
◉	Sights	p100
⊗	Eating	p102
⊗	Drinking	p105
⊕	Entertainment	p107
⊕	Shopping	p107

400 m
0.2 miles

El Poblenou Beaches

Platja de
Bogatell

Platja de la
Nova Icària

Parc del
Poblenou

Cementiri del
Poblenou

EL POBLENOU

Rambla del
Poblenou

Poblenou Ⓜ

SANT
MARTÍ

Museu
Can Framis

Torre
Glòries

Museu del
Disseny de
Barcelona

Glòries Ⓜ

Plaça de
les Glòries
Catalanes

Llacuna Ⓜ

Bogatell Ⓜ

Espacio
88

Universitat
Pompeu
Fabra

Parc de
Carles I

Parc de la
Ciutadella

Monumental Ⓜ

EL
FORT
PIENC

Gran Via de les
Corts Catalanes

Arc de
Triomf Ⓜ

Barceloneta, the Waterfront & El Poblenou

MEDITERRANEAN SEA

Port Olímpic

Plaça dels Voluntaris

C de Trelawny

● Peix

LA BARCELONETA

C de Balboa

C de la Sal

C de la Maquinista

C del Baluard

C de la Ginebra

C de Sant Carles

29 ⊗14

C del Mar

⊗ 12

15 ⊗

C del Mar

Barceloneta Ⓜ

Pg de Joan de Borbó

Moll de la Barceloneta

Plaça de Pau Vila

27 ●

●2 Museu d'Història de Catalunya

Marina

7 Portes

Pla de Palau

⊗21

⊗ 25

24 ⊗

Pg d'Isabel II

El Cap de Barcelona

Moll d'Espanya

PORT VELL

Mirador del Port Vell

Port Vell

0 ———— 200 m
0 ———— 0.1 miles

F

E

Platja de la Barceloneta Ⓐ

Parc de la Barceloneta

Pg de Salvat Papasseit

Pg del Doctor Aiguader

Ciutadella Ⓜ Vila Olímpica

Zoo de Barcelona

Estació de França Ⓡ

Pg de Circumval·lació

Av del Marquès de l'Argentera

Pg de Picasso

LA RIBERA

C de la Princesa

EL BORN

Jaume I Ⓜ

C de Jaume I

Via Laietana

BARRI GÒTIC

C de Jaume I

LA BARCELONETA

C de Balboa

C de la Ginebra

C del Baluard

C del Mar

Pg de Joan de Borbó

Platja de la Barceloneta

Pg de Martín de la Barceloneta

C d'Andrea Doria

Platja de Sant Miquel ●

Molokai SUP Center

● L'Estel Ferit

C de Guitert

C Atlàntida

C de l'Escar

Plaça del Mar

Homenatge a la Natació

Club Natació Atlètic-Barceloneta

Sea You 🏬

Barceloneta Ⓜ

Marina

PORT VELL

Mirador del Port Vell

See Enlargement

Moll d'Espanya

Port de Barcelona

Pg de Colom

Ronda del Litoral

Plaça del Portal de la Pau

Rambla de Mar

Drassanes Ⓜ

●1 Museu Marítim

Plaça de les Drassanes

A   B   C   D   5 6 7 8

Sights

Museu Marítim
MUSEUM

1 ◉ MAP P98, A8

The city's maritime museum occupies the mighty Gothic Reials Drassanes (Royal Shipyards) – a remarkable relic from Barcelona's days as the seat of a seafaring empire. Highlights include a full-scale 1970s replica of Don Juan de Austria's 16th-century flagship, fishing vessels, antique navigation charts, dioramas of the Barcelona waterfront, and a life-sized replica of the *Ictíneo I*, one of the world's first submarines, invented in 1858 by Catalan polymath Narcís Monturiol. (www.mmb.cat)

Museu d'Història de Catalunya
MUSEUM

2 ◉ MAP P98, E7

Within the revitalised 1880s **Palau de Mar**, this excellent multimedia museum travels through 2000 years of Catalan history, from the Stone Age to the arrival of Modernisme and the Spanish Civil War (touching heavily on the cultural and political repression felt across Catalonia postwar), and into the 21st century. (www.mhcat.cat)

Museu del Disseny de Barcelona
MUSEUM

3 ◉ MAP P98, C1

Nicknamed *la grapadora* (the stapler), Barcelona's fascinating design museum lies inside a monolithic contemporary

El Cap de Barcelona, by Roy Lichtenstein

building with a brutalist appearance. Inside, it houses a dazzling collection of ceramics, fashion, decorative arts and textiles, and is a must for anyone interested in the design world. Almodóvar film posters, ceramics by Picasso and Miró, 16th-century French ballgowns and haute couture from the 20th and 21st centuries (including pieces by Spanish designer Cristóbal Balenciaga) count among the many highlights. (www.museudeldisseny.cat)

Rambla del Poblenou   STREET

4 MAP P98, E2

With its origins in the mid-19th century (when Poblenou's industrial boom kicked off), this leafy boulevard has long been the neighbourhood hub, sprinkled with tapas bars, cafes and restaurants, and flanked by a few Modernista buildings.

Museu Can Framis   MUSEUM

5 MAP P98, D1

Set in an 18th-century former textile factory converted by local architect Jordia Badia, this light-flooded contemporary gallery showcases Catalan painting from the 1960s onwards. Displays are regularly refreshed, and might include the dreamlike sequences of Perejaume, the complex work of Antoni Tàpies, the beautifully textured creations of Josep

Seaside Sculptures

The waterfront area hosts an array of intriguing street sculptures, most notably **Peix** (Map p98, D5), Frank Gehry's shimmering, bronze-coloured, 35m-tall headless fish facing the Port Olímpic, from 1992. Other works include the Port Vell's 1992 **El Cap de Barcelona** (Map p98, D7) by Roy Lichtenstein; Rebecca Horn's 1992 tribute to the old waterfront shacks, **L'Estel Ferit** (Map p98, C7); and Alfredo Lanz's 2004 **Homenatge a la Natació** (Map p98, C8).

Guinovart, bold pieces by self-taught Modest Cuixart, and Agustí Puig's ethereal *Menines*. (www.fundaciovilacasas.com)

Torre Glòries   ARCHITECTURE

6 MAP P98, C1

Barcelona's famously cucumber-shaped tower, Jean Nouvel's luminous 38-storey Torre Glòries is among the most daring additions to the skyline since the first towers of La Sagrada Família went up. The building's top floors have been transformed into a viewing platform, with an installation by Argentinian artist Tomás Saraceno set into its dome; the lift zips up 30 floors in 34 seconds. (www.miradortorreglories.com)

Barceloneta, the Waterfront & El Poblenou Sights

Espacio 88   ARTS CENTRE

7 ◉ MAP P98, C2

Hosting everything from yoga classes to pop-up boutiques to flower markets, this white-walled, concrete-floored warehouse-like space puts the art centre stage, with dynamic events and exhibitions. Also here is the uberpopular **Skye coffee truck** (www.skye-coffee.com; 📶). (www.espacio88.com)

Eating

Can Recasens   CATALAN €€

8 ✖ MAP P98, E1

One of El Poblenou's most romantic settings, century-old Can Recasens conceals a warren of warmly lit rooms full of oil paintings, flickering candles, fairy lights and fruit baskets. The food is outstanding, with a mix of salads, smoked meats, fondues, and *torrades* (toasted bread) topped with delicacies such as smoked-salmon carpaccio. Local *cava*, Catalan wines and vermouths make the perfect complements. (www.canrecasens.restaurant)

Little Fern Café   CAFE €

9 ✖ MAP P98, D1

Worth a trip out to Poblenou in itself, this beautiful Kiwi–Hungarian-owned cafe has white-brick walls, floor-to-ceiling windows and plants in terracotta pots, along with original all-day-brunch bites fired with organic ingredients, such as fluffy corn fritters with smashed avocado. There are also sunny mimosas,

Barcelona-made Caravelle craft beers and local Three Marks coffee (p128). (www.littleferncafe.com; 📶)

Can Fisher   SEAFOOD €€

10 ✖ MAP P98, F3

Overlooking Platja del Bogatell, Can Fisher is locally loved for its divine rice and seafood dishes, served in a beach-chic setting and prepared using fresh, organic, locally sourced ingredients. Paellas here are kept thin, letting the rice shine in the style of classic Costa Brava cooking – try the grilled-mushroom paella, the black rice with cuttlefish or the wood-fired rice with scarlet shrimp. (www.canfisher.com; 📶 ✖)

Xiringuito Escribà   SEAFOOD €€€

11 ✖ MAP P98, F3

The family team behind Escribà, which has been making sweets since 1906, is also in charge of one of Barcelona's unmissable waterfront seafood-and-rice restaurants, beside Platja del Bogatell. A whirl of busy staff and bubbling paellas, this is one of the few places in town that does one-person paella or Catalan *fideuà*, as well as delicious vegetarian-friendly options. Finish off with Escribà pastries. (www.xiringuitoescriba.com; ✖)

Can Solé   SEAFOOD €€€

12 ✖ MAP P98, F8

Behind imposing wooden doors, Barceloneta's elegant oldest restaurant has been serving terrific seafood since 1903, with white-cloth tables, white-jacketed waiters and photos of celebrity customers. Freshly landed catch stars in traditional dishes such as *arròs caldòs* (brothy seafood rice) and 'grandmother'-style dishes like *sarsuela* (fish-and-seafood casserole). (www.restaurantconsole.com)

Els Pescadors   SEAFOOD €€€

13 🍽 MAP P98, F2

On a picturesque square lined with low houses and long-established South American *bella ombre* trees, this delightful family restaurant serves some of the city's best fish and seafood-and-rice dishes. Three indoor dining areas include the main old-tavern room; on warm nights, tables outside are a joy. The focus is on fuss-free classic cooking – seasonal rices and stews, and oven-baked fish. (www.elspescadors.com; 🛜)

Bodega La Peninsular   TAPAS €

14 🍽 MAP P98, F7

At this traditional-style bodega with a marble-topped bar, artfully presented tapas are chalked up on blackboards to pair with house-made vermouth and Catalan vintages. Adhering to the Slow Food ethos, ingredients are organic, seasonal and locally sourced or homemade. Try the *mojama* (salt-cured tuna), the renowned *bombes* with tangy aioli, or a giant wedge of tortilla. (www.tabernaycafetin.es)

Active Waterfront

○ **Watersports** Catch the sunrise from a paddleboard with **Molokai** (Map p98, C7; www.molokaisupcenter.com) or **Sea You** (Map p98, C8; https://seayoubarcelona.com); both also do SUP yoga, surfing and more.

○ **Club Natació Atlètic-Barceloneta** (Map p98, C8; www.cnab.cat) Warm and cool lap pools next to La Barceloneta at this 1907-founded club.

○ **Yoga** Regular classes happen each week, including **Yoga by the Sea** (www.yogabytheseabarcelona.com).

Can Ros   SEAFOOD €€€

15 🍽 MAP P98, F8

A fifth generation now leads this immutable 1908-opened seafood favourite. In a restaurant where the decor recalls simpler times, there's a straightforward guiding principle: juicy fresh fish (from the Barceloneta docks) cooked with a light touch, along with rich seafood rices and *fideuà* with cuttlefish. The weekday lunch *menú* includes rice for one (a rarity). (www.canros.cat)

Can Dendê   BREAKFAST €

16 🍽 MAP P98, E2

All-day brunch is the culinary star at Poblenou's bohemian Brazilian-run Can Dendê. Tuck into eggs Benedict with smoked salmon,

Insider Knowledge: Unmissable Catalan Restaurants

Moments (www.mandarinoriental.com) Chef Raül Balam offers a creative, contemporary gastronomy inspired by local ingredients and Catalan culture at the Mandarin Oriental Barcelona's two-Michelin-star restaurant.

7 Portes (Map p98, D6, https://7portes.com; 📞) With 185 years of history, this not-to-be-missed spot specialises in dishes from Catalonia's culinary tradition, as well as paellas and other rices.

Els Pescadors (p103) At this century-old El Poblenou restaurant, Marc Maulini prepares Catalan-style cuisine that revolves around the freshest seafood and fish.

La Gormanda (Map p120, B3; https://lagormanda.com; Carrer d'Aribau 160) Young chef Carlota Claver goes for innovative, market-fresh cooking based on Catalan classics, in L'Eixample.

Bodega Sepúlveda (Map p166, D1; www.bodegasepulveda.com; Carrer de Sepúlveda 173) A Sant Antoni favourite led by the Solà family, with traditional Catalan cuisine and over 70 years on Barcelona's food scene.

Recommended by Carme Ruscalleda, *award-winning chef and culinary advisor of Moments restaurant; find on Instagram @carme.ruscalleda*

fluffy savoury pancakes or pulled-pork sandwiches, accompanied by a mimosa or homemade pink lemonade, to a soundtrack of Latin Tropicalia and American grooves. (www.candende.com)

Leka
INTERNATIONAL €€

17 🍴 MAP P98, D2

Cooking up vegetables from its own garden, organic meats from responsible Pyrenees producers and seafood from Barceloneta's markets and the Delta de l'Ebre, Leka gets crammed for its generous weekday lunch *menú*. Thoughtfully prepared options swing from portobello-and-chickpea burgers to veg-and-mushroom rice and seaweed fritters. (https://restauranteleka.com; 📝)

El 58
TAPAS €

18 🍴 MAP P98, E2

With a marble bar and original artwork, this lively French–Catalan fave serves imaginative, beautifully prepared seasonal tapas – braised tuna with *salsa romesco* (tomato and pepper sauce) and asparagus, fried aubergines with honey and rosemary and sausage-and-chickpea stew. (www.facebook.com/el58poblenou)

Minyam
SEAFOOD €€

19 MAP P98, E1

Billowing beneath a tajine-like metal lid, smouldering herbs infuse the rice of Minyam's signature Vulcanus (smoked paella). Tapas dishes at this stylish, contemporary Poblenou restaurant are equally original, including steamed mussels with ginger and apple, and honeyed aubergine tempura with lime. (www.facebook.com/minyamcisco)

Més de Vi
TAPAS €

20 MAP P98, F2

At this buzzing Poblenou wine-and-tapas bar, drops from Costers del Segre, Empordà and other Catalan DO (Denominació d'Origen) regions are accompanied by delicious, inventive *platillos* (shared plates), such as courgette carpaccio, Iberian-ham croquettes and citrus-marinated salmon. Brick walls, timber tables and studded Chesterfield sofas give it a cosy ambience. (www.restaurantemesdevi.es)

Green Spot
VEGETARIAN €€

21 MAP P98, E6

Battered cauliflower with tamarind-and-mint sauce, quesadillas with kimchi and avocado and jackfruit tacos are among

the inventive vegetarian, vegan and gluten-free dishes created from seasonal ingredients. It's all presented in a stylish, minimalist dining room with beautiful white-washed vaulted ceilings. (www.encompaniadeloboss.com;)

Els Tres Porquets
TAPAS €

22 MAP P98, D1

Tiles cover the walls, shelves burst with wine bottles (many organic and natural) and the tradition-inspired menu is chalked up on the board in this warm tavern-style tapas bar at the far-northern end of Poblenou's *rambla*. Market-fresh dishes change with the seasons, from artisanal cheeses to *ous estrellats* (fried eggs) with chorizo. (https://elstresporquets.es)

Drinking

Frutas Selectas
COFFEE

23 MAP P98, D2

Poblenou's beloved and minimalist branch of Nømad (p89), started by top barista Jordi Mestre, brews seasonal, fairtrade beans. From expertly served cold brews to perfect flat whites, coffee is serious business here, with pastries on the side. (www.nomadcoffee.es)

Perikete
WINE BAR

24 MAP P98, D7

A fabulous wine spot between El Born and Barceloneta proper that's always jam-packed with both *barcelonins* and visitors.

Jabugo hams hang from the ceiling, vermouth barrels sit above the bar and wine bottles (over 200 varieties) cram every available shelf space. Excellent tapas include made-to-order tortilla and grilled prawns. (www.gruporeini.com)

Bodega Vidrios y Cristales

WINE BAR

25 🚇 MAP P98, D6

In the history-steeped, stone-floored 1840 Casa Xifré building, this atmospheric little jewel recreates an old-style neighbourhood bodega with tins of sardines, anchovies and other delicacies lining the shelves (and used in exquisite tapas). House-made vermouth and a wonderful array of wines are the thing. (www.gruposagardi.com)

Balius

COCKTAIL BAR

26 🚇 MAP P98, E1

There's an old-fashioned jauntiness to Poblenou's vintage-style cocktail den Balius, marked by its original-period tiled exterior. Staff pour classic cocktails, vermouths and G&Ts; Sundays have live jazz; and there's a small tapas menu (cheeses, olives). (www.baliusbar.com)

BlackLab

MICROBREWERY

27 🚇 MAP P98, E7

Barcelona's original brewhouse, within the 19th-century Palau de Mar (p100), serves 16 house-made craft beers, including saisons, double IPAs and dry stouts. American brewmaster Matt Boder is constantly experimenting, the kitchen sizzles up Asian–American bites (burgers, dumplings, ramen), and one-hour tours (book ahead) take you behind the scenes. (www.blacklab.es)

Van Van Var

BAR

28 🚇 MAP P98, C3

The shoebox-sized permanent bar of hit street-food market **Van Van** hosts regularly changing food-truck chefs, which means there's steaming ramen one week and home-cooked falafel the next, along with classic tinned tapas. The sunny terrace is perfect for a Catalan wine, a classic vermouth or a chilled beer. (www.vanvanmarket.com)

La Violeta

WINE BAR

29 🚇 MAP P98, F7

A regularly changing line-up of natural wines, both Spanish and international, wanders into the spotlight at this cosy bar with tables on Barceloneta's market square. Exciting Catalan picks accompany lovingly made slow-food tapas starring home-grown vegetables, Ebro Delta oysters, burrata-and-tomato salad and artisanal cheeses. (www.facebook.com/lavioletavinosnaturales)

La Cervecita Nuestra de Cada Día
CRAFT BEER

30 MAP P98, E2

Equal parts beer shop and craft-brew bar, minimal-decor La Cervecita has a changing selection of at least 15 unique beers on tap from around Europe and the US. You might stumble across a Catalan sour fruit beer, a rare English stout or a potent Belgian triple ale. (www.facebook.com/lacervecitanuestradecadadia)

Entertainment

Razzmatazz
LIVE MUSIC

31 ⭐ MAP P98, C2

Bands from far and wide occasionally create scenes of near-hysteria at Razzmatazz, one of the city's classic live-music and clubbing venues. Five different rooms, in one huge postindustrial space. (www.salarazzmatazz.com)

Shopping

Mercat dels Encants
MARKET

32 🔒 MAP P98, B1

In a gleaming open-sided complex, the 'Market of Charms' is Barcelona's biggest flea market, and one of Europe's oldest, with its roots in medieval times. More than 300 vendors ply their wares beneath massive mirror-like panels. There are several morning auctions each week, and the top floor hosts food stalls for croquettes, *pintxos* (Basque tapas) and more. (Fira de Bellcaire; https://encantsbarcelona.com)

Palo Market Fest
MARKET

33 🔒 MAP P98, F1

One of the city's most-loved events, festival-vibe Palo Market takes over an old Poblenou warehouse, wreathed in flowers and greenery, once a month. Local artisans set up stalls alongside sizzling street-food trucks and lively vermouth bars. (https://palomarketfest.com)

Mercat del Poblenou
MARKET

34 🔒 MAP P98, F2

Designed in 1889 by Pere Falqués and originally a livestock market (though now sensitively remodelled), Poblenou's fresh-produce market bursts with Catalan cheeses, meats, fruit, veg and home-cooked meals. (http://mercatpoblenou.com)

Mercat del Clot
MARKET

35 🔒 MAP P98, C1

The elegant Modernista market of untouristed El Clot (just north of Poblenou) was first opened in 1889. Now thoughtfully restored, it overlooks a leafy square lined by cafes and restaurants. (www.mercatdelclot.net)

Explore

L'Eixample & La Sagrada Família

Filled with broad, grid-like boulevards, elegant L'Eixample is a showcase for Barcelona's great Modernista architecture, including Gaudí's still-unfinished masterpiece, La Sagrada Família. It's a busy, sprawling area split in two halves (Esquerra and Dreta), with an upmarket dining scene, chic boutiques and diverse nightlife, much of it centred on the buzzing LGBTIQ+ clubs of the 'Gaixample'.

The Short List

○ **La Sagrada Família (p110)** *Seeing history being made at Spain's most-visited monument and Gaudí's greatest (still unfinished) legacy.*

○ **La Pedrera (p114)** *Wandering through this rippling Gaudí masterpiece or catching a concert on the rooftop.*

○ **Casa Batlló (p116)** *Marvelling at the swirling, almost-alive facade of this Gaudí-designed home with wave-shaped window frames and balconies.*

○ **Divine dining (p124)** *Jumping into the varied food scene, from bistro-style Besta to Michelin-star Disfrutar.*

○ **Fundació Antoni Tàpies (p122)** *Deciphering the fascinating contemporary art of leading 20th-century Catalan artist Antoni Tàpies.*

Getting There & Around

Ⓜ Catalunya, Passeig de Gràcia, Diagonal, Tetuan and Girona are useful metro stops. Línies 2 and 5 stop at Sagrada Família.

🚈 Plaça Catalunya and Provença are served by FGC trains.

Neighbourhood Map on p120

La Sagrada Família (p110) ALEXANDER SPATARI/GETTY IMAGES ©

Top Experience

Marvel at Gaudí's Spectacular Sagrada Família

Gaudí's Unesco-listed Sagrada Família inspires awe by its sheer verticality. Despite work beginning in 1882, it's still under construction, though it's hoped it will be completed in time for its 150th anniversary in 2032. With 4.5 million annual visitors, this is Spain's most visited monument. Rich in iconography, and at once ancient and modern, La Sagrada Família leaves no one unmoved.

◉ MAP P120, F1

www.sagradafamilia.org

A Holy Mission

The Temple Expiatori de la Sagrada Família (Expiatory Temple of the Holy Family) was Antoni Gaudí's all-consuming obsession. Given the commission by a conservative society that wished to build a temple as atonement for the city's sins of modernity, Gaudí saw its completion as his holy mission. As funds dried up, he contributed his own. In all, he spent 43 years on La Sagrada Família, after taking over from the original architect Francisco de Paula del Villar y Lozano in 1883.

Gaudí devised a temple 95m long and 60m wide, able to seat over 13,000 people, with a central tower 172.5m high above the transept (representing Christ) and another 17 towers of 100m or more. At Gaudí's death, only the crypt, the apse walls, one portal and one tower had been finished. Work began again in 1952, but controversy has always clouded progress. Opponents of the continuation of the project claim that the computer models based on what little of Gaudí's plans survived the anarchists' ire during the Spanish Civil War have led to the creation of a monster that has little to do with Gaudí's plans and style.

The Interior, the Apse & the Crypt

The roof is held up by a forest of innovative, extraordinary angled pillars that soar towards the ceiling, sprouting a web of supporting branches and creating the effect of a forest canopy. The stained glass, divided in shades of red, blue, green, yellow and ochre, creates a hypnotic, magical atmosphere when the sun hits the windows.

Underneath the apse, glass windows reveal the simple neo-Gothic **crypt** below, where Gaudí was buried on 12 June 1926. Built from 1882–89, the crypt is the oldest part of the entire structure and largely the work of Gaudí's predecessor, Villar. Mass is now held here

★ Top Tips

o All tickets must be booked online and include a download-able app audioguide. There are 50-minute guided tours, and you can also book trips (by lift and stairs) up the towers.

o Hats, see-through clothing, low neck-lines and exposed backs/midriffs/ shoulders aren't permitted. Shorts and skirts must be at least mid-thigh.

o Don't miss nearby Recinte Modernista de Sant Pau (p122) and, for a taste of local life, the **Mercat Sagrada Família**.

✕ Take a Break

Blackbird serves delicious speciality coffee, **Can Pizza** (http://canpizza.eu; 🖉) is perfect for gour-met pizzas and low-key **Celler Miquel** (www.facebook.com/ CellerMiquel) does vermouth, *cava* and wine.

Or wander 800m south to local hangout Passeig de Sant Joan (p131), for vermouth, brunch and more.

and it's open only during hours of worship.

Nativity Facade & Claustre del Roser

The northeastern Nativity Facade (Façana del Naixement) is the artistic pinnacle of the building, mostly created under Gaudí's personal supervision. The four towers are destined to hold tubular bells capable of playing complex music at great volume. The portal represents, from left to right, Hope, Charity and Faith, and is a forest of sculpture (Gaudí used plaster casts of local people). At the top is a green cypress tree, the refuge in a storm for the white doves of peace dotted over it.

To the right of the facade is the curious Claustre del Roser, a Gothic-style mini-cloister tacked onto the outside of the church; its 1897-completed portal is considered to be a guide by Gaudí to future builders.

Passion Facade & Schools of Gaudí

The southwest Passion Facade (Façana de la Passió), on the theme of Christ's last days and death, was built between 1954 and 1978, based on surviving drawings by Gaudí, with four towers and a large, sculpture-bedecked portal – but was only officially completed in 2018. The late sculptor Josep Maria Subirachs (1927–2014) worked on its decoration from 1986 to 2006. He did not attempt to imitate Gaudí, instead producing angular, controversial images of his own. The main series of sculptures, on three levels, are in an S-shaped sequence, starting with

La Sagrada Família, exterior detail

Antoni Gaudí

Antoni Gaudí i Cornet (1852–1926) was born in either Reus or nearby Riudoms village (there's some debate), trained initially in metalwork, and obtained his architecture degree in Barcelona in 1878. He was a devout Catholic, a Catalan nationalist and an almost lifelong vegetarian. Although part of the Modernisme movement, Gaudí had a style all of his own. The architect's work is an earthy appeal to sinewy movement, yet often with a dreamlike or surreal quality, eliminating straight lines. A recurring theme was his obsession with the harmony of natural forms. The lines between real and unreal, sober and dreamdrunk are all blurred, and the grandeur of his vision was matched by an obsession with detail.

With age he became almost exclusively motivated by stark religious conviction, and from 1915 he gave up all other projects to devote himself exclusively to La Sagrada Família. When he died in June 1926 (he was knocked down by a tram on Gran Via de les Corts Catalanes), less than a quarter of La Sagrada Família had been completed.

the Last Supper at the bottom left and ending with Christ's burial at the top right.

Immediately in front of the Passion Facade, the Schools of Gaudí (Escoles de Gaudí) was constructed as a children's school in 1909, using the traditional Catalan vault and with an undulating classic-Gaudí brick roof that brings to mind La Pedrera (p114).

Glory Facade & Central Towers

Gaudí wanted the Glory Facade (Façana de la Glòria) – the basilica's eventual main entrance, facing Carrer de Mallorca – to be the most magnificent facade. Like the three others, it will be crowned by four towers; all 12 towers together represent the Twelve Apostles. Inside will be the narthex, a kind of foyer made up of 16 'lanterns', a series of hyperboloid forms topped by cones. It's expected to be the final section to reach completion.

The northwestern end of the building revolves around six central towers. The first of these six, the 138m-high Torre de la Mare de Déu, was finished in late 2021 and is topped by an enormous 12-pointed star – the first tower to be completed in over 40 years. Four of the six central towers will symbolise the Four Evangelists, reaching 135m high. They will all surround the massive 172.5m central tower above the transept, representing Christ (and with a lift zipping up inside). Further decoration will make the whole building a microcosmic symbol of the Christian church, and almost as tall as Montjuïc mountain.

Top Experience 📷

Be Dazzled by Gaudí's La Pedrera

In the top tier of Gaudí's achievements, this madcap Unesco-listed masterpiece, with 33 balconies, was built between 1905 and 1910 as a combined apartment and office block. Formally called Casa Milà, after the businessman who commissioned it, it's better known as La Pedrera (the Quarry) because of its uneven grey stone facade, which ripples around the corner of Carrer de Provença.

◉ MAP P120, D2

Casa Milà

www.lapedrera.com

Facade & Patios

When commissioned to design La Pedrera, Gaudí wanted to top anything else done in L'Eixample (including adding parking space). The natural world was one of the most enduring influences on Gaudí's work, and the building's undulating grey-stone facade evokes a cliff face sculpted by waves and wind. The wave effect is emphasised by elaborate wrought-iron balconies that bring to mind seaweed washed up on the shore. The lasting impression is of a building on the verge of motion – a living building.

The two unique patios (where visits begin) flood the apartments with natural light and were treated by Gaudí like interior facades, with wrought-iron balconies, nature-inspired murals and a bridge-like, almost-floating staircase. It might feel impossible, but a handful of people still live at La Pedrera.

El Pis de la Pedrera & Espai Gaudí

Below the attic, the elegantly furnished apartment is done up in the style that a well-to-do family might have enjoyed in the early 20th century. The sensuous curves, rippling distribution and unexpected touches in everything from light fittings to bedsteads, from door handles to balconies, might seem admirable to us today, but not everyone thought so at the time.

One floor below the roof, the attic feels like the fossilised ribcage of some prehistoric beast, with 270 parabolic brick arches. It hosts a small museum with intriguing models of Gaudí's creations.

Roof Terrace

Gaudí's blend of mischievous form with ingenious functionality is evident on La Pedrera's rooftop, where clusters of chimneys, stairwells and ventilation towers rise and fall on the structure's wave-like contours. Some are unadorned, others are decorated with *trencadís* (ceramic fragments) and even broken *cava* bottles.

★ Top Tips

○ Buy tickets online (saving €3 on most ticket types) to avoid the worst of the crowds; standard tickets include a videoguide. The Unseen Pedrera guided tours include otherwise off-limits spaces such as the car park.

○ La Pedrera hosts superb open-air performances on the roof in summer; check in advance.

○ Don't miss the restored ochre-hued rear facade, which you can also often see by popping into the back of the shop at Passeig de Gràcia 96.

✕ Take a Break

A 300m walk southwest of La Pedrera, **La Bodegueta Provença** (www.labodeguetaprovenza.com; 🛜) serves first-rate tapas and wines.

Or head 700m southwest to Auto Rosellon (p127) for garden-fresh *menús* and other delights.

Top Experience 📸

Get Lost in the Beauty of Casa Batlló

One of Europe's strangest residential buildings, Casa Batlló (built 1904–06) is Gaudí at his fantastical best. From its playful facade, awe-inspiring rooftop and marine-world inspiration to its revolutionary experiments in light and architectural form (straight lines are few and far between), this apartment block is one of the most beautiful buildings in a city where the architectural stakes soar sky-high.

◉ MAP P120, E4

www.casabatllo.es

The Facade

To Salvador Dalí, Casa Batlló's facade resembled 'twilight clouds in water'. Others see a resemblance to the impressionist masterpiece *Water Lilies* by Claude Monet. It's certainly exquisite and whimsical, sprinkled with fragments of blue, mauve and green tiles, and studded with wave-shaped window frames and mask-like balconies that look like the bony jaws of some strange beast – hence the nickname *casa dels ossos* (house of bones).

Sala Principal

The internal light wells shimmer with tiles of deep-sea blue. Gaudí eschewed the straight line, so the spiral staircase wafts you up to the 1st floor. In the main salon (often called the Sistine Chapel of Modernisme), the ceiling twists into a whirlpool-like vortex around its sun-like chandelier; the doors, windows and skylights are dreamy waves of wood and coloured glass in mollusc-like shapes. The sense of light and space here is extraordinary, thanks to the wall-length window looking out on to Passeig de Gràcia.

Back Terrace & Roof

Pass the interior courtyard (with its pale-blue cascading wave) to Casa Batlló's back terrace: a fantasy garden in miniature, opening on to an expansive L'Eixample inner patio. The accumulation of more than 300 *trencadís* have the effect of immersing you in a kaleidoscope. In the attic, see Gaudí's trademark hyperboloid arches.

With its twisting chimney pots so characteristic of Gaudí's structures, the roof is Casa Batlló's grand crescendo. It was built to look like the shape of an animal's back, with shiny scales – the 'spine' changes colour as you walk around. The eastern end represents Sant Jordi (St George) and the Dragon; another local name for Casa Batlló is the *casa del drac* (house of the dragon).

★ Top Tips

o Buy tickets online (which also saves a few euros) and go first thing or in the evening. Be the First tickets get you in at 8.30am before general opening.

o The Batlló family's 20th-century private residence on the 1st floor has been restored; it's included in Gold tickets (otherwise there's an additional charge to visit it).

o During summer months, concerts are staged under the stars on the magical rooftop.

✗ Take a Break

Just 300m away, off the east side of Passeig de Gràcia, Tapas 24 (p126) is one of Barcelona's most innovative tapas bars.

Or head 600m west to **Baldomero** (www.casabaldomero.com), a stylish pink-walled cafe-restaurant inspired by a traditional Catalan *masía* (country home).

Walking Tour 🥾

More Modernisme in L'Eixample

When the Catalan architect Ildefons Cerdà's revolutionary plan to create the new neighbourhood of L'Eixample came into swing from the 1860s onwards, the city's top Modernista architects got to work all over the district. Beyond Gaudí's headliners, L'Eixample is crammed with Modernista creations by Lluís Domènech i Montaner, Josep Puig i Cadafalch, Enric Sagnier and others. The street-facing facades are often highlights.

Walk Facts

Start Casa Sagnier; Ⓜ Diagonal

End Palau Macaya; Ⓜ Verdaguer

Length 2km; one to two hours

❶ Casa Sagnier

Dating from 1892, the home and professional studio of Modernista architect Enric Sagnier i Villavecchia is a vision of Gothic-inspired elements, ornamental sculpture and vast windows on the upper floors; it now houses a stylish **boutique hotel** (https://hotelcasasagnier.com) with a cafe-restaurant.

❷ Casa Serra

At Casa Serra (built 1903–08), Josep Puig i Cadafalch let his imagination loose on a neo-Gothic whimsy with a central tower topped by a conical roof. Artists Eusebi Arnau and Alfons Juyol added the facade's busts: famous faces from Miguel de Cervantes to Marià Fortuny.

❸ Casa Comalat

A striking twin-fronted building with vibrant tilework, Casa Comalat was created from 1909 to 1911 by Salvador Valeri (1873–1954), with obvious Gaudí influences on the main facade (the wavy roof and bulging balconies). Carrer de Còrsega has the more playful facade, with its uneven wooden galleries and windows stacked like cards.

❹ Palau Baró de Quadras

Puig i Cadafalch redesigned this 1882 residential building (https://casessingulars.com) in exuberant Gothic-inspired style, with two distinct facades (the main one with emotive gargoyles and reliefs), between 1902 and 1906. Interior visits are by prebooked tour only.

❺ Palau Ramon Montaner

Though notable for its exterior and its leafy gardens, Lluís Domènech i Montaner's 1893 Palau Ramon Montaner is especially spectacular on the inside (open only by sporadic guided tour). The interior is laden with sculptures (some by Eusebi Arnau), mosaics, fine woodwork and a grand staircase beneath an ornamental skylight.

❻ Casa Thomas

One of Domènech i Montaner's earlier efforts, completed in 1912, Casa Thomas has trademark floral motifs and reptile figurines, and the massive ground-level wrought-iron decoration is magnificent.

❼ Casa Llopis i Bofill

An interesting 1902 block of flats designed by Antoni Gallissà (1861–1903), Casa Llopis i Bofill has an eye-catching graffiti-covered, oriental-inspired facade, while the elaborate parabolic arches on the ground floor and wrought-iron balconies are typically Modernista.

❽ Palau Macaya

Just north stands Puig i Cadafalch's 1901 Palau Macaya (https://macaya.caixaforum.org), one of Barcelona's least-known Modernisme gems. Beyond the bright-white facade, the interior has a grand entrance, an open courtyard decked in colourful tiles and a delicately carved marble staircase.

L'Eixample & La Sagrada Família

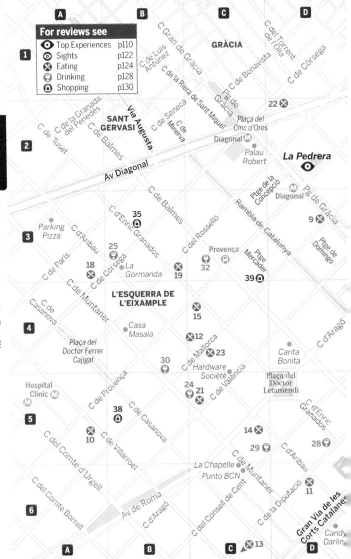

For reviews see

GRÀCIA

SANT GERVASI

L'ESQUERRA DE L'EIXAMPLE

La Pedrera

Diagonal M

Palau Robert

Parking Pizza

La Gormanda

Casa Masala

Hardware Société

Plaça del Doctor Ferrer Cajigal

Hospital Clínic M

La Chapelle Punto BCN

Plaça del Doctor Letamendi

Carita Bonita

Candy Darling

Plaça del Cinc d'Oros

Av Diagonal

Via Augusta

Av de Roma

Gran Via de les Corts Catalanes

E

C del Rosselló

C de Bailèn

F

G

H

La Sagrada Família
2

Casa de
les Punxes
6

Verdaguer
M

Av Diagonal

C de Roger de Flor

C de Nàpols

1

C de Girona
40

C de Provença

C de Mallorca

C de València

C d'Aragó

Pg de Sant Joan

Granja
Petitbo

Chichalimoná

El Viti

Parking
Pizza

2

C de Roger de Llúria

C del Bruc

Mercat de la
Concepció
5

C de Pau Claris

34

36

Basílica de la
Puríssima Concepció
i Assumpció de
Nostra Senyora

C del Consell de Cent

20

C de Bailèn

Plaça de
Tetuan

Girona
31
M

Funky
Bakers
Eatery

Tetuan
M

3

LA DRETA DE
L'EIXAMPLE

C de la Diputació

17

C de Casp

C de Girona

Passeig de
Gràcia
M

1

Casa Batlló
3

Casa Amatller

4

Casa Lleó
Morera

16

33

Gran Via de les Corts Catalanes

C de Roger de Llúria

26

C del Bruc

27

8

Casa
Calvet

C d'Ausiàs Marc

4

Fundació
Antoni
Tàpies
7

C de Pau Claris

C de Casp

Ronda de
Sant Pere

Arena
Madre

Arena
Classic

Rambla de Catalunya

Jardins de
la Reina
Victòria

Pg de Gràcia

Plaça
d'Urquinaona

Urquinaona

Ronda de
Sant Pere

Urquinaona
M

C de Trafalgar

C de les Jonqueres

5

Universitat de
Barcelona
37

7

Plaça de la
Universitat

C de Balmes

Ronda de la
Universitat

Catalunya
M

Plaça de
Catalunya

C de Fontanella

Via Laietana

Universitat
M

C de Bergara

C de Pelai

Catalunya
M

La Rambla
M

BARRI
GÒTIC

6

C dels Tallers

EL RAVAL

Ronda de Sant Antoni

E

F

C de Santa Anna

Av del Portal de l'Àngel

C Comtal

G

N

0   200 m
0   0.1 miles

H

Sights

Fundació Antoni Tàpies
GALLERY

1 ◉ MAP P120, E4

The major collection of leading 20th-century Catalan artist Antoni Tàpies (who died aged 88 in 2012) is also a pioneering 1880s Modernista building, designed by Domènech i Montaner for publishers Editorial Montaner i Simón. Known for his esoteric work, Tàpies left behind over 2000 powerful paintings and a foundation intended to promote contemporary artists. The building combines a brick-covered iron frame with Islamic-inspired decoration, all crowned by Tàpies' installation *Núvol i cadira* (Cloud and Chair). (www.fundaciotapies.org)

Recinte Modernista de Sant Pau
ARCHITECTURE

2 ◉ MAP P120, F1

Domènech i Montaner outdid himself as architect and philanthropist with the Modernista Hospital de la Santa Creu i de Sant Pau. Built between 1902 and 1930, it was long considered one of Barcelona's most important hospitals, but was repurposed into cultural centres, offices and a monument in 2009. A joint Unesco World Heritage Site with the Palau de la Música Catalana (p84), the 27-building complex is lavishly decorated (tiling, stained glass, arches) and each of its 16 pavilions unique. (www.santpaubarcelona.org)

Casa Amatller
ARCHITECTURE

3 ◉ MAP P120, E4

One of Puig i Cadafalch's most striking flights of Modernista fantasy, Casa Amatller combines Gothic window frames and Romanesque flourishes with a stepped gable borrowed from Dutch urban architecture. Busts and reliefs of dragons, knights and other characters drip off the main facade. The building was renovated in 1900 for chocolate baron and philanthropist Antoni Amatller (1851–1910), and now also houses Modernisme-influenced jeweller **Bagués-Masriera** (www.bagues-masriera.com). (www.amatller.org)

Casa Lleó Morera
ARCHITECTURE

4 ◉ MAP P120, E4

Domènech i Montaner's 1905 contribution to the Illa de la Discòrdia has Modernista carving outside and a bright tiled lobby in which floral motifs predominate. It's now occupied by luxury fashion store **Loewe** (www.loewe.com).

Mercat de la Concepció
MARKET

5 ◉ MAP P120, F2

Dating from 1888 (though remodelled in 1998), Dreta de L'Eixample's elegant iron-clad market was envisioned by

Taking in Barcelona's Modernisme

Barcelona's flamboyant Modernisme buildings emerged during the late 19th century, a period of great artistic and political fervour deeply connected to Catalan identity, which transformed early-20th-century Barcelona into a showcase for avant-garde architecture. Leading the way was Antoni Gaudí (see p113). Aiming to establish a new Catalan archetype, Gaudí and other visionary architects drew inspiration from the past – shapes, details and brickwork reminiscent of Islamic, Gothic and Renaissance designs.

Materials & Decorations

Modernista architects relied on artisan skills that have now been all but relegated to history. Stone, unclad brick, exposed iron and steel frames, and the copious use of stained glass and ceramics, were all features of the new style. The craftspeople required for these tasks were the heirs of the guild masters.

Other Architects

Lluís Domènech i Montaner (1850–1923) and Josep Puig i Cadafalch (1867–1956) left a wealth of remarkable buildings across Barcelona, while the Rome-trained sculptor Eusebi Arnau (1863–1933) was one of the most popular figures called upon to decorate Barcelona's Modernista piles, including the Hospital de la Santa Creu i de Sant Pau, the Palau de la Música Catalana (p84) and Casa Amatller.

Antoni Rovira i Trias. It's particularly loved for its flower shops. (www.laconcepcio.cat)

Casa de les Punxes ARCHITECTURE

6 ◉ MAP P120, E1

Resembling a medieval castle, Puig i Cadafalch's 1905 Casa Terrades is known as the Casa de les Punxes (House of Spikes) because of its pointed tile-adorned turrets. It's now a coworking space. (Casa Terrades)

Universitat de Barcelona ARCHITECTURE

7 ◉ MAP P120, E6

Although a university was first set up on what is now La Rambla in the 16th century, the present glorious mix of (neo) Romanesque, Gothic, Islamic and Mudéjar architecture is a caprice of the 19th century (by Ildefons Cerdà's friend, Elies Rogent). Wander the main hall, the cloisters and the water-laced **Jardins Ferran Soldevilla**. (www.ub.edu)

Casa Calvet

ARCHITECTURE

8 MAP P120, G4

Gaudí's most conventional (though still intricately detailed) contribution to L'Eixample is the 1900 Casa Calvet, an early commission for textiles industrialist Pere Màrtir Calvet, inspired by baroque tendencies.

Eating

Lasarte

MODERN EUROPEAN €€€

9 MAP P120, D3

One of Barcelona's preeminent restaurants – and its first to gain three Michelin stars (in 2017) – Lasarte is overseen by lauded chef Martín Berasategui and headed up by Paolo Casagrande. From pickled oysters with hibiscus and white garlic to red-mullet *suquet* (fish stew) with smoked sardines, this is seriously sophisticated, seasonally inspired cookery, served in an ultra-contemporary dining room. (www.restaurantlasarte.com)

Disfrutar

GASTRONOMY €€€

10  MAP P120, A5

Two-Michelin-star Disfrutar (means 'Enjoy' in English) ranks among the city's finest restaurants. Run by alumni of Ferran Adrià's game-changing El Bulli, nothing is as it seems, such as black and green olives that are actually chocolate ganache with orange-blossom water. The Mediterranean-inspired decor

Universitat de Barcelona (p123)

by Catalan designers El Equipo Creativo is fabulously on point, and service is faultless. The team's 2022-opened **Compartir Barcelona** (www.compartirbarcelona.com) is similarly a showstopper. (www.disfrutarbarcelona.com; 🖾)

Mont Bar
BISTRO €€€

11 🔣 MAP P120, D6

Named for owner Iván Castro's Val d'Aran hometown, this Michelin-star space with black-and-white floors, bottle-lined walls, over 250 wines and a smart terrace offers next-level cooking fired by organic, seasonal ingredients, many of them home-grown. Exquisite tapas and small plates come courtesy of ex-Tickets chef Fran Agudo – ceviche 'snacks', cockle soufflé, tuna belly with pine-nut emulsion. Next door **Mediamanga** (www.mediamanga.es; 🖾) is also superb (same team!). (www.montbar.com; 🛜 🖾)

Besta
FUSION €€

12 🔣 MAP P120, C4

The fruits of both the Atlantic and Mediterranean infuse the ambitious, weekly-changing menu devised by a Galician–Catalan chef duo at this hot bistro-inspired arrival, with an irresistible Spanish-wines menu. Fresh seafood stars in creative, boundary-pushing dishes – seaweed falafel, roasted carrots with caviar, Betanzos-style tortilla with octopus. The team is also behind similarly fabulous **Batea** (https://bateabarcelona.com). (https://bestabarcelona.com)

Cinc Sentits
CATALAN €€€

13 🔣 MAP P120, C6

Enter the realm of the 'Five Senses' to indulge in jaw-dropping eight- or 10-course seasonal tasting menus of small experimental dishes concocted by chef Jordi Artal (no à la carte, although dishes can be tweaked on request). The use of fresh local produce, such as Costa Brava line-caught fish and top-quality Extremadura suckling pig, is key at this Michelin-star address. (www.cincsentits.com; 🖾)

Pepa
TAPAS €€

14 🔣 MAP P120, C5

An old bookshop graced by original check-tiled floors is the setting for outstanding, inventive *platillos* (sharing plates). Don't miss the mushroom carpaccio with strawberries and wasabi vinaigrette, the fabulous eggs with chips and truffle or langoustines, the deliciously fresh tomato-and-fig salad, and more. Desserts are just as exquisite, while wines are natural, organic and biodynamic. (www.facebook.com/PepaBaraVins; 🖾)

Gresca
CATALAN €€

15 🔣 MAP P120, C4

Everything revolves around the open-plan kitchen at elegant, unmissable, bistro-inspired Gresca. Chef Rafa Peña specialises in ambitious reinterpretations of quality seasonal produce, combined with exclusively natural wines that change weekly. Try beetroot salad

International Flavours

Funky Bakers Eatery (Map p120, G2; https://funkybakers.com) From just-baked babkas and perfect coffee to meze platters, Middle Eastern-inspired Funky Bakers is an all-day, organic-rooted delight.

Casa Masala (Map p120, B4; www.casamasala.es) One of Barcelona's top Indian restaurants, with organic-fired street-food dishes (green-veg korma, vindaloo tacos) and lunchtime thalis.

Hardware Société (Map p120, C4; www.hardwaresociete.com) The third outpost of this creative Melbourne-born cafe brings divine Aussie-style brunches and Market Lane coffee to L'Eixample.

with Greek yoghurt, aubergine in parmesan cream or a *bikini* (toastie) with chanterelle mushrooms.

You can also try Peña's culinary creations until late in gourmet-sandwich style at nearby green-clad **Bar Torpedo** (https://bartorpedo.com). (www.gresca.rest; 🍴)

Tapas 24   TAPAS €

16 🍴 MAP P120, F4

Hotshot chef Carles Abellán runs this basement tapas haven known for its gourmet renditions of old faves, including the

bikini, here with truffle and cured ham, freshly cooked tortilla and zesty lemon-infused *boquerones* (anchovies). You can't book, but it's worth the wait. Before 1pm, pop in for superb *entrepans* (filled rolls) and omelettes. Also on Diagonal (p156). (www.carlesabellan.com; 🛜)

Bodega Bonay   ITALIAN €€

17 🍴 MAP P120, H3

The freshest local produce, creative Italian flavours and exclusively natural wines steal the show at this lively, rustic-chic bodega, hidden away in the artily converted 19th-century **Casa Bonay** (www.casabonay.com; ❄ 🛜) building. Chef Giacomo Hassan's tempting menu changes seasonally, from gnocchi drenched in rich *salvia* sauce to falafel with labneh. Also here are cocktail bar Libertine (p129) and rooftop El Chiringuito. (www.casabonay.com)

Brugarol X   TAPAS, FUSION €€€

18 🍴 MAP P120, A3

In an on-the-up foodie pocket of Esquerra de L'Eixample, Catalan–Japanese beauty Brugarol fuses tapas and izakaya bars to perfection. Inventive delights such as tamarind oysters, slow-cooked duck and crispy mushroom or tuna tartare wonton are created using organic Costa Brava produce, including olive oil, goat's cheese and wines from the owners' own fincas. Also in the Barri

Gòtic (p50). (www.brugarolbarcelona.com)

Auto Rosellon

INTERNATIONAL €€

19 MAP P120, B3

With cornflower-blue paintwork and fresh produce on display, Israeli chef Ronit Stern's popular restaurant-cafe works organic ingredients sourced from small producers and from its own garden into creative dishes like roasted beetroot with goat's cheese and burrata with pumpkin and pears. There are natural wines, homemade juices, cocktails, craft beers and a weekday *menú*. (www.autorosellon.com; 🛜 🍴)

Betlem

TAPAS €

20 MAP P120, G2

Within a beautifully repurposed 1892 building with rust-red trim and lovely tiling, this laid-back neighbourhood gastrobar specialises in artfully prepared yet uncomplicated market-based tapas and *platillos* (sharing plates). Pick from platters of cold meats and local cheeses, seasonal tortilla, chunky *patates braves* and stuffed *entrepans* to go with your vermouth, *cava* or Catalan wine. (www.betlem.es; 🍴)

Taktika Berri

PINTXOS €€

21 MAP P120, C5

Reservations are essential at smart, family-owned Taktika Berri, a part-bar, part-restaurant favourite serving some of the best *pintxos* (Basque tapas) in town. Morsels like blood sausage, gooey tortilla, smoked salmon or *bacallà* (salt cod) are snapped up as soon as they arrive fresh from the kitchen. (www.taktikaberri.net)

Entrepanes Díaz

TAPAS €

22 MAP P120, D2

Gourmet sandwiches, from roast beef to the favourite crispy squid with squid-ink aioli, are the highlight at this sparkling old-style bar, along with Spanish sharing plates such as battered sea urchins, prawn fritters and Barbastro-tomato salad. The charming team also runs wonderful **Bar Mut** (www.barmut.com) across the road. (www.facebook.com/EntrepanesDiaz)

Tapas 24

MARGARET STEPHEN/LONELY PLANET ©

Albé

MEDITERRANEAN €€

23 ⊗ MAP P120, C4

A fabulous blend of Catalan and Lebanese flavours awaits at gastrobar-style Albé. Seasonal ingredients sourced from local producers shine in irresistible creations like baked cauliflower with toasted butter, aubergine with a pomegranate reduction and beautifully spiced mackerel with avocado *leben* (yoghurt). It's all served in a cosily chic, moodily lit space. (www.albebarcelona.com)

Drinking

Sips

COCKTAIL BAR

24 ⊙ MAP P120, C5

With two top mixologists at the helm (Simone Caporale and Marc Álvarez), it's no surprise that cutting-edge Sips landed a spot on the World's 50 Best Bars list in 2021. Innovative cocktails such as the signature Espresso Martini (with whipped cream) are expertly mixed at hands-on stations among the tables and forest-green decor. (http://sips.barcelona)

Dry Martini

COCKTAIL BAR

25 ⊙ MAP P120, B3

The expertly mixed house martini, enjoyed at the gleaming wooden bar or the plush green banquettes, is always a good bet – over a million are thought to have been served here. Dry Martini is a smart, dimly lit, old-style space, with bottle-filled cabinets and original artwork. (www.drymartiniorg.com)

Three Marks

COFFEE

26 ⊙ MAP P120, H4

Catalan–Italian-owned by, yes, three Marks, this is a split-level stripped-back speciality-coffee corner with a cosy neighbourhood vibe on the untouristed Fort Pienc side of L'Eixample. Flat whites and espresso made with beans roasted in Barcelona go perfectly with the creative sandwiches. (https://threemarkscoffee.com)

La Textil

CRAFT BEER

27 ⊙ MAP P120, G4

Stylish brewpub, lively music venue and superb local-produce restaurant all rolled into one, La Textil has over 20 craft beers on tap, including its own creations, along with natural Catalan wines. The food dazzles too, with rich smoked or grilled dishes (such as carrots with ginger cream) from the flowy open-plan kitchen. (www.latextil.beer)

Satan's Coffee Corner

COFFEE

Find home-baked pastries and Japanese-inspired, street-food-style bites to pair with devilishly delicious seasonal coffee (beans by local roaster Right Side) at this white-walled speciality cafe tucked into the chic Casa Bonay (see 17 Map p120, H3) hotel. There's another branch (p53) in the Barri Gòtic. (https://satanscoffee.com)

Cosmo
CAFE

28 🚇 MAP P120, D5

Just behind the university, this cool cafe/cultural space has hanging bicycles and bright splashy murals. Most ingredients are homemade or from the neighbourhood, with fresh juices, arty brunches, home-baked cakes and speciality coffee, not to mention beer, wine and weekend mojitos. (www.galeriacosmo.com)

Garage Beer Co
CRAFT BEER

29 🚇 MAP P120, C5

One of the original craft-beer bars to pop up in Barcelona, Garage brews its own, and offers around 10 different styles at a time. The Ocata (a delicate session IPA), Soup (a more robust IPA) and Circus Tears (an Imperial stout) are favourites. (www.garagebeer.co)

Hemingway
COCKTAIL BAR

30 🚇 MAP P120, B4

There's often a queue out the door for a table at this intimate, speakeasy-style basement cocktail den with a tiny front terrace. International whiskies, rare gins and imaginative, artfully presented cocktails crafted with fresh-pressed citrus juices are owner and bartender Luca Izzo's specialities. (http://hemingwaybcn.com)

Local Tips: Favourite Haunts 🍴

Norte (www.facebook.com/norterestaurante) Perfect at lunchtime or breakfast – simple home-style food, like eating at the house of a friend who is a great cook.

Gresca (p125) By chef Rafa Peña, with wonderful small plates to share, made using seasonal produce, and an incredible wine selection.

Parking Pita Some of the best filled pitas in Barcelona; the bread is made using the same pizza dough as popular Parking Pizza (p131), with which it shares a space.

Sato i Tanaka (https://satotanaka.com) One of Barcelona's top Japanese counters, serving elegant, excellent-value tasting menus courtesy of a chef duo.

Libertine Cocktail Bar (p126) At Casa Bonay's lobby bar, everything is made in-house, from bitters to fermentations. A place in which to mingle with local creatives over dinner and cocktails.

 Recommended by Inés Miró-Sans, *founder of Casa Bonay hotel; find on Instagram @casabonay*

L'Eixample & La Sagrada Família Drinking

Cafè del Centre

BAR

31 🚇 MAP P120, G3

In business since 1873, this Modernista cafe-bar has been glammed up (without losing its character) by the nightlife experts behind El Raval's La Confiteria (p68). Settle in among the check-print floors, mahogany bar and marble-topped tables for classic vermouth or cocktails by top mixologist Andreu Estríngana. (www.facebook.com/cafedelcentre1873; 🛜)

Mediterráneo

BAR

32 🚇 MAP P120, C3

A range of quality (free) live music and comedy is staged almost nightly at student favourite 'El Medi'. (www.elmedi.net)

Visiting the Gaixample

The area just north of Gran Via de les Corts Catalanes and to the west of Rambla de Catalunya, popularly known as the 'Gaixample', is the heart of Barcelona's LGBTIQ+ scene, with bars, clubs, restaurants and a lively buzz. Popular haunts include Candy Darling (p29), La Chapelle (p29), Arena Madre (p29), Arena Classic (p29), Punto BCN (p29) and Carita Bonita (p29).

Shopping

Carner Barcelona

PERFUME

33 🔒 MAP P120, F4

Set within a beautifully converted protected building with white-brick vaulted ceilings, Carner crafts irresistible scents inspired by Barcelona and the Mediterranean, all vegan, cruelty-free and locally made with a focus on the environment. The miniature sets make perfect take-home treats. (https://carnerbarcelona.com)

Flores Navarro

FLOWERS

34 🔒 MAP P120, F2

Established in 1960, this vast, soothing florist never closes, and has two spaces on Carrer de València, bursting with everything from sky-blue roses to potted palms. (www.floristeriasnavarro.com)

TheAvant

FASHION & ACCESSORIES

35 🔒 MAP P120, B3

Barcelonin designer Silvia Garcia Presas creates her elegant women's dresses, shirts, shoes and other fashion pieces by working directly with local producers, and has a soothing collection of artisanal homewares at the Primitiu branch a few doors down. (www.theavant.com)

Joan Múrria

FOOD & DRINKS

36 🔒 MAP P120, E3

Ramon Casas designed the 1898 Modernista shopfront adverts at

Drinking and Dining in Passeig de Sant Joan

A long, leafy boulevard in eastern L'Eixample, Passeig de Sant Joan has morphed into a fashionable drinking-and-dining pocket.

○ **Parking Pizza** (Map p120, H2; www.parkingpizza.com; 🍴) Sprawling warehouse cooking up outrageously popular wood-fired pizzas and pita; also has a **branch** (Map p120, A3) just off Diagonal.

○ **Granja Petitbo** (Map p120, G1; www.granjapetitbo.com; 📶🍴) This sunny corner cafe has an all-day local-produce menu and terrific coffee.

○ **Chichalimoná** (Map p120, G2; www.chichalimona.com; 📶) Loved for its global-inspired plates, weekend brunches and vermouth-hour bites.

○ **El Viti** (Map p120, H2; www.elviti.com; 📶) A vermouth bar with a nouveau-tavern vibe and inventive tapas.

this culinary temple of speciality foods from around Catalonia and beyond. Artisan cheeses, Iberian hams, olive oils, *cavas* and wines, coffee and loose-leaf teas are among the treats. (Queviures Múrria; www.murria.cat)

Altaïr   BOOKS

37 🔒 MAP P120, E5

Enter a travel wonderland at this extensive bookshop, founded in 1979, which has enough guidebooks, maps, travel literature, noticeboards and other goodies to fuel all your world-wandering dreams. (www.altair.es; 📶)

Mercat del Ninot   MARKET

38 🔒 MAP P120, B5

A gleaming, modern, working neighbourhood market, on the site of a 19th-century open-air predecessor that was covered in 1933,

the Mercat del Ninot reopened in 2015 after a five-year makeover, retaining its original metal structure. It sells everything from meat and fish to just-baked bread and fresh fruit, and has a couple of cafe-bars. (www.mercatdelninot.com; 📶)

La Central   BOOKS

39 🔒 MAP P120, C3

An excellent multilingual bookshop with titles stocked amid lovely old tiled floors, and a speciality terrace cafe. (www.lacentral.com)

La Vinícola   WINE

40 🔒 MAP P120, F2

As-local-as-possible labels are the stars at this temple to Catalan grapes, styled like a smartened-up bodega storeroom. There's a keen focus on exquisite wines from northern Catalonia. (www.lavinicola.cat)

Explore ⊚
Gràcia & Park Güell

An independent town until the 1890s, Gràcia is awash with narrow lanes, scattered plazas and old-time businesses that still have a village-like charm. Well-worn cafes, eco-conscious shops and a thriving food-and-drink scene draw a lively crowd, while cultural jewels include the fantastic Casa Vicens, designed by Gaudí. To its north lies Gaudí's outdoor storybook, Park Güell.

The Short List

○ **Park Güell (p134)** *Savouring the otherworldly sculptures, mosaics and columns of Gaudí's open-air wonderland, and enjoying the hillside views.*

○ **Village squares (p136)** *Wandering between Gràcia's many charming squares and dipping into the eco-friendly independent boutiques.*

○ **Casa Vicens (p139)** *Admiring the interplay of brick, floral motifs, chequerboard patterns and Moorish elements at this Unesco-listed Gaudí castle-mansion.*

○ **Mercat de la Llibertat (p139)** *Shopping for delectable local specialities at this emblematic market.*

○ **Vermouth hour (p144)** *Joining the fer el vermut fun at a timeworn vermouth bar or a revamped bodega.*

Getting There & Around

Ⓜ Línia 3 to Diagonal, Fontana or Lesseps and Línia 4 to Joanic are best.

Foot Strolling northwest along Passeig de Gràcia from Plaça de Catalunya is a lovely way to reach the neighbourhood (1.5km walk, 25 minutes).

Neighbourhood Map on p138

Plaça de la Vila de Gràcia (p137) KAUKA JARVI/SHUTTERSTOCK ©

Top Experience 📷
Explore Magical Park Güell

At the Unesco-listed Park Güell, Gaudí turned his imagination to landscape gardening. It's a surreal, enchanting place where the Modernista's passion for natural forms really took flight, to the point where the artificial almost seems more normal than the natural. Eusebi Güell hired Gaudí to create this miniature city for the wealthy in 1900, on a tree-covered hillside (then outside Barcelona), though the project was abandoned in 1914.

◎ MAP P138, A1

www.parkguell.barcelona

A Wild Space

Before Gaudí, the 20-hectare hillside was filled with vines, olive trees and orchards. Today, it's a fragrant expanse of oaks, pines, wisteria, olive groves, magnolias, lavender and rosemary, with an ongoing focus on replanting autochthonous species. Much of the park is still wooded, but laced with pathways. The best views are from the cross-topped **Turó de les Tres Creus** (Turó del Calvari) in the southwest corner.

Plaça de la Natura & Sala Hipóstila

Begin at the broad, open **Plaça de la Natura**, at the top of the monumental complex. The Plaça doubles as a rainwater catchment area and its centrepiece is the 1914 **Banc de Trencadís**. Curving sinuously around the perimeter, this multicoloured tiled bench was designed by architect Josep Maria Jujol (1879–1949). To the west of the square extends the **Pòrtic de la Bugadera** (Laundry Room Portico), a gallery where the twisted stonework columns and roof give the effect of a cloister beneath tree roots – a recurring motif.

Beneath the square, opposite two immediately recognisable Hansel-and-Gretel houses and the typically curvaceous **Casa del Guarda**, steps lead past a much-photographed mosaic dragon/lizard to the **Sala Hipóstila** (Doric Temple), with its tiled ceilings and Catalan vaults. This forest of 86 stone columns – some leaning like mighty trees bent by the weight of time – was originally intended as a market.

Casa-Museu Gaudí

Near the park's eastern entrance lies the spired dusty-pink **Casa-Museu Gaudí** (https://sagradafamilia.org), where Gaudí lived for the last 20 years of his life (1906–26). The house was built in 1904 by Francesc Berenguer i Mestres as a prototype for an intended 60 houses, and is now filled with Gaudí-designed furniture and ironwork.

★ **Top Tips**

○ As part of ongoing renovations and efforts to reclaim the park for local residents, visitor ticket numbers have been reduced – book ahead (including guided tours).

○ The park is a 20-minute walk from Lesseps or Vallcarca metro stops; the uphill trek is eased by escalators. Buses H6 and D40 stop on Travessera de Dalt, a 10-minute walk south (with escalators). Bus V19 stops at the eastern entrance.

○ Visit the northern part of the park (the *zona forestal*, without the Gaudí features) free of charge.

✕ **Take a Break**

Stop at La Panxa del Bisbe (p141) in upper Gràcia for delicious tapas and good wines.

Or wander further down into Gràcia for seafood tapas at Lluritu (p141) or vermouth and *conserves* (canned seafood) at Vermuteria del Tano (p144).

Walking Tour

Gràcia's Village Squares

Gràcia was a separate village until 1897, and its tight, narrow lanes and endless interlocking squares still retain their village-like feel. In places bohemian, in others gentrified, Gràcia is Barcelona at its most eclectic, its nooks and crannies home to everything from soulful old taverns to eco-minded boutiques. The neighbourhood squares are liveliest in the evening and during Sunday vermouth hour.

Walk Facts

Start Ⓜ Diagonal metro station

End Plaça del Nord; Ⓜ Lesseps

Length 2km; two hours

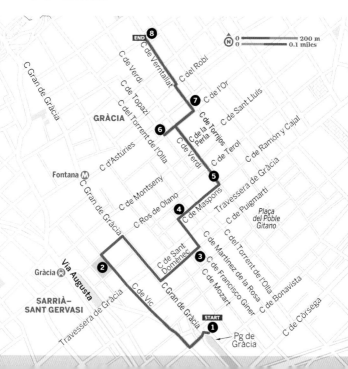

❶ Casa Fuster

Head north into Gràcia proper, where you'll find a grand Modernista edifice now turned sumptuous hotel, Casa Fuster (www.hotelcasafuster.com; P ❄ 🛜 ♒), designed by Domènech i Montaner between 1908 and 1911.

❷ Plaça de la Llibertat

Lively Plaça de la Llibertat is home to Gràcia's main fresh-produce market (a Modernista beauty) and a couple of great little restaurants. The market was designed by Gaudí's protégé, Francesc Berenguer i Mestres.

❸ Vila de Gràcia

Meandering east, you'll find the popular Plaça de la Vila de Gràcia, fronted by the local town hall, which was also designed by Berenguer. At the square's heart stands the 1864 **Torre del Rellotge** (Clock Tower), created by Antoni Rovira i Trias, the Catalan architect behind the Sant Antoni, La Concepció and El Born markets.

❹ Plaça del Sol

Just north lies the rowdiest of Gràcia's squares, Plaça del Sol, where bars and restaurants come to life and people congregate on the steps. The square was the scene of summary executions after an uprising in 1870, and, during the civil war, an air-raid shelter was installed.

❺ Plaça de la Revolució de Setembre de 1868

This busy elongated square commemorates the toppling of Queen Isabel II, a cause of much celebration in this working-class stronghold. Long-running **Bar Canigó**, founded in 1922 and now overseen by a third generation of owners, is an animated spot for house vermouth or coffee.

❻ Plaça del Diamant

Buzzy Plaça del Diamant hosts a couple of cafe-bars and a 12m-deep bomb shelter from the civil war (open only by guided Sunday tour; https://guia.barcelona.cat). Also here is Xavier Medina-Campeny's bronze statue *La Colometa*, which recalls the protagonist of celebrated Catalan writer Mercè Rodoreda's novel *La plaça del Diamant*.

❼ Plaça de la Virreina

Pleasant terraces adorn the leafy, pedestrianised Plaça de la Virreina, presided over by the 19th-century **Església de Sant Joan**, another piece by Berenguer. Some people believe that the interior chapel is the work of Gaudí himself, though the jury is still out.

❽ Plaça del Nord

Towards the top of the *barri*, this shaded northern square has a laid-back local feel, with cafe tables, neighbours chatting on benches and kids racing around the little playground.

A **Park Güell** ⦿
C d'Olot

B
Bunkers
del Carmel

C 0   400 m
N 0   0.2 miles

D

1

C de Mariano

C de Larrard

⦿ 3

Av del Coll
del Portell

For reviews see		
⦿ Top Experiences	p134
⦿ Sights	p139
⊗ Eating	p140
⊜ Drinking	p144
✪ Entertainment	p146
🔒 Shopping	p147

2

Travessera de Dalt

⊗ 8
C del Torrent de les Flors
C de Rabassa
C de Ca l'Alegre de Dalt
C de l'Escorial

Plaça de
Lesseps

C de Sant Salvador
C de Martí
Plaça de
Rovira
i Trias
⊗ 6

Plaça
del Nord
C de Verntallat

3
C de Pérez Galdós
C del Torrent de l'Olla
C de Verdi
C del Robí
Plaça de
la Virreina
C del Torrent d'En Vidalet
C de Joan Blanques

GRÀCIA

C de Montmany
C de Sant Lluís
C de Pi i Margall

Joanic
Ⓜ

Casa
Vicens
⦿ 1
C de les
Carolines

26 ⊜   21 ⊜
C de l'Or
C de Ramón y Cajal
Pg de
Sant Joan

4
24 ⊜
C de la Perla
C de Torrijos
⊗ 23
Travessera de Gràcia
Ⓜ Fontana
28 ✪
C de Vallfogona
15 ⊗
⊜ 20
C de Bailèn
Ⓐ 31

Rambla
de Prat
34 🔒
C de Montseny
C de Ros de
Olano
Plaça de la Revolució
de Setembre de 1868
C de Puigmartí
⊗⊜ 13
⊗ 14
22 ⊜
C de Mila i Fontanals
C de Tordera
C de
Banyoles

Bodega
Neus
C de Berga
33 🔒
C del
Planeta
25 ⊜
C de Siracusa
C de la Llibertat

5
30 🔒
7 ⊗
Mercat de
la Llibertat
⊗ 2
La Vermu ⊜
⊗ 11
C del Progrés
C del Perill

Gràcia 🚉
Ⓐ 4
Plaça de
Gal·la
Placídia
9 ⊗   16 ⊗
18 ⊜
⊜ 29
C de Mariá Cubí
C de Vic
C de Goya
C de Mozart
C del Torrent de l'Olla
C de Martínez de la Rosa

SANT
GERVASI
10 ⊗
C de la Riera de Sant Miquel
19 ⊜
C de Francisco
Giner

17 ⊜
C de Luís
Antúnez
Pg de Gràcia
Ⓐ 35
🔒 32
C de Bonavista
C de Santa
Teresa
C de Córsega

6
Via Augusta
Travessera de Gràcia
C de Balmes
C de
Séneca
⊗ 5
C de Minerva
⊗ 12
Av Diagonal
C de Roger
de Llúria
C de Pau
Claris

A   B   C Ⓜ Diagonal   D

Sights

Casa Vicens
ARCHITECTURE

1 ◉ MAP P138, A4

A Unesco-listed masterpiece, this angular, turreted 1885-completed summer house was Gaudí's inaugural commission, at age 30, created for stock and currency broker Manuel Vicens i Montaner. The richly detailed facade is awash with ceramic colour and shape, including distinctive marigold tiling based on the site's original gardens. As frequently seen, Gaudí sought inspiration from the past, in this case the rich heritage of building in the Mudéjar-style brick, typical in parts of Spain conquered by the Christians from the Moors – note the tinkling fountain overlooking the courtyard. (www.casavicens.org)

Mercat de la Llibertat
MARKET

2 ◉ MAP P138, A5

Opened in 1888, the 'Market of Liberty' was covered in 1893 by Francesc Berenguer i Mestres (1866–1914), Gaudí's long-time assistant, in typically fizzy Modernista style, employing generous whirls of wrought iron. Despite a considerable facelift in 2009, it remains emblematic of Gràcia: full of life, laughter and fabulous fresh produce, and with irresistible tapas spots like **El Tast de Joan Noi** and **La Clau**. (www.facebook.com/elmercatdelallibertat)

Casa Vicens

MARCO FINE/SHUTTERSTOCK ©

An Architect's Eye: Gaudí in Detail

Park Güell (p134) The Sala Hipóstila's pillars support a flat plaza with wavy ceramic benches above – the whole thing works as a water filter.

Pavellons Güell (p154) Gaudí designed the dragon entry gate and stables for the Güell estate in Pedralbes; the orange atop the column recalls the dragon-guardian of Hesperides Garden.

Casa Vicens (p139) Gaudí's first house, for a tile manufacturer, in Gràcia. The palm-leaf fence foreshadows the natural forms in his future work.

Palau Güell (p63) The beginning of Gaudí's structural experiments, this Raval mansion has a spiral staircase, Catalan vaults and his signature broken-tile rooftop chimneys.

Cripta Gaudí (www. gaudicoloniaguell.org) The culmination of Gaudí's structural innovations, at the Colònia Güell west of Barcelona. Each porch column represents a different tree.

Recommended by Pia Wortham, *architect and guide at Barcelona Architecture Walks; find on Instagram @barcelonarchitecturewalks*

Parc del Turó del Putxet

PARK

3 MAP P138, A1

Fragrant with Mediterranean pines and rosy-pink oleanders, this peaceful forested hill park rises to 178m, just northeast of upper Gràcia, opening up dazzling 360-degree views of the city.

Eating

La Pubilla

CATALAN €€

4 ✖ MAP P138, B5

Hidden away by the Mercat de la Llibertat, from where many ingredients are sourced, chef Alexis Peñalver's La Pubilla specialises in hearty *'esmorzars de forquilla'* (fork breakfasts) beloved by local residents. There's an outrageously popular daily three-course *menú*, which stars updated-Catalan dishes such as baked cod, fig gazpacho with mozzarella and squid-and-mushroom rice. Book ahead.

The team also runs tiny **Extra Bar** (www.lapubilla.cat), serving memorable season-rooted *platillos* (sharing plates).

Berbena

MEDITERRANEAN €€

5 ✖ MAP P138, B6

Tucked away off busy Diagonal, Berbena specialises in ambitiously prepared, beautifully presented seasonal dishes from its open-plan kitchen. The daily-changing *menú* starts with home-baked bread and sides of tortilla, accompanied by a main such as fennel-and-mushroom rice or beef tongue with smoked

Taking in the View at Bunkers del Carmel

On the Turó de la Rovira hill in El Carmel neighbourhood, the **Bunkers del Carmel platforms** (Turó de la Rovira; Map p138, B1; www. bunkers.cat) have magnificent 360-degree Barcelona panoramas. Part of an anti-aircraft battery during the Spanish Civil War, this spot was a shanty town until the early 1990s, and has lain abandoned since then. But its popularity with both *barcelonins* and visitors has skyrocketed in recent years, leading to growing local complaints about noise, partying and other antisocial behaviour. At the time of writing, access is restricted to daylight hours only; check locally and, if visiting, be respectful of residents. Welcoming hillside restaurant **Las Delicias** (www.barrestaurantedelicias.com; Carrer de Mühlberg 1) makes a great pitstop for tapas and grilled meats.

aubergines. It's a tiny, minimalist-modern space, with seats in the window. (www.berbenabcn.com; 📍)

Lluritu   SEAFOOD €€

6 🗺 MAP P138, C3

From salted sardines to king prawns, perfectly grilled, un-adorned bites fresh from the ocean are the order of the day at this self-styled *desenfadada* (casual) seafood restaurant, deco-rated with a marble bar. Prized ingredients for the short, select menu are sourced from all along the Spanish coast, but especially Catalonia. There's also a second branch, **Lluritu 2**. (www.lluritu.com)

Botafumeiro   SEAFOOD €€€

7 🗺 MAP P138, B5

A wonderfully smart world of Galician seafood, Botafumeiro has long been a magnet for VIPs visit-ing Barcelona. It's a good place to

try *percebes* (goose barnacles), the ultimate fruit-of-the-sea deli-cacy. You can bring the price down by sharing a few *mitges racions* (large tapas plates), such as cod fritters and L'Escala anchovies. (www.botafumeiro.es)

La Panxa del Bisbe   TAPAS €€

8 🗺 MAP P138, C2

With its local buzz and artfully min-imalist interior, the well-established 'Bishop's Belly' in upper Gràcia delivers creative season-inspired tapas that earn high praise from both *barcelonins* and visitors. Feast on provolone-stuffed courgette flowers, grilled octopus with capers and celery, or *cap i pota* (beef-and-chickpea stew) with a twist. (📶 📍)

Kibuka   JAPANESE €€

9 🗺 MAP P138, B5

Gràcia's most-loved Japanese haunt gets packed for its uber-fresh

CLAUDIOVALDES/SHUTTERSTOCK ©

Vermouth with appetisers

maki prepared with a touch of creativity, from Italian *uramaki* (with mozzarella, asparagus and basil oil) to Mexican-inspired rolls (salmon ceviche and chipotle salsa), as well as classics like spicy tuna or avocado. Also on lively **Carrer de Verdi**. (www.kibuka.com)

Bar Bodega Quimet   TAPAS €

10 🍴 MAP P138, B6

A relic from a bygone age, now lovingly managed by a pair of brothers, this is a delightfully atmospheric spot, with old bottles lining the walls, marble tables, tiled floors and a burnished wooden bar backed by house-vermouth barrels. The lengthy tapas list specialises in *conserves* (canned seafood), but also turns out cheese

platters and fresh anchovies and octopus.

Baby Jalebi   PUNJABI €

11 🍴 MAP P138, C5

Perfectly spiced pakoras and samosas, paneer or chicken tikka masala, aloo tikki burgers and fragrant vegetable biryani are just a few of the street-food temptations at this creative Punjabi favourite. It's all served with pillowy tandoor-fresh naan and contemporary flair, in an industrial-feel space with beamed ceilings and neon lighting. Also in Sant Antoni.

Les Filles   CAFE €€

12 🍴 MAP P138, B6

Both gorgeous design space and buzzing garden café-restaurant,

Les Filles is adorned with pine-green booths, vases of fresh flowers and jazzy cushions and rugs. Rooted in fresh, seasonal flavours and organic ingredients, dishes take a health-focused turn, with options like Pyrenees trout, quinoa-and-veg bowls, lentil salads and creative weekend brunches. (www.lesfillesbarcelona.com;)

Cal Boter   CATALAN €€

13 MAP P138, D4

Families and high-spirited groups of pals are drawn to this classic for *cargols a la llauna* (sautéed snails), *botifarra* (Catalan sausage) with beans, roast lamb, seasonal soups and other Catalan specialities, rustled up amid marble tables and green-washed doors. The three-course week-day *menú* is good value. (www.restaurantcalboter.com)

La Fonda Pepa   CATALAN €€

14 MAP P138, D4

Beamed ceilings, a metallic bar and marble-top tables set the informal tone for gourmet, market-driven Catalan cooking, in a building that was once a neighbourhood *casa de menjars* (meals house). Sizzling seafood *arrossos* (rices), *patates braves* with home-made sauce, citrus-marinated sea bass and perfect grilled artichokes might pop up on the menu, and wines are from small Catalan vineyards. (www.fondapepa.com)

Pepa Tomate   TAPAS €€

15 MAP P138, C4

Dressed in tomato-reds, this casual tapas spot with a few coveted terrace tables keeps busy at all hours. Fresh produce from the local markets fuels the wide-ranging menu, with elegantly presented dishes such as baked aubergine with goat's cheese, grilled asparagus with burrata, or *patates braves* with a kick. (www.pepatomategrup.com;)

Peaceful Horta

At the foot of the Collserola hills, the peaceful northern neighbourhood and former village of Horta has a lively square (Plaça d'Eivissa), ancient *masíes* (country farmhouses) and an 18th-century garden. Laid out by Italian engineer Domenico Bagutti, the carefully manicured **Parc del Laberint d'Horta** (www.barcelona.cat; Passeig del Castanyers 1) remained private until the 1970s; now, with its cypress-edged labyrinth, it's a perfect escape. Combine with a meal at a centuries-old *masía*, such as **Can Travi Nou** (www.gruptravi.com; Carrer de Jorge Manrique 8) with its seasonal menus or **Can Cortada** (www.cancortada.com; Avinguda de l'Estatut de Catalunya;) with its Catalan specialities.

Enjoying Gràcia's Vermouth Bars

Bodega Neus (Map p138, A5) Popular, rustic-modern *vermuteria* near the market, which also does fabulous tapas (truffled tortilla, sweet-potato *braves*, *esqueixada*).

La Vermu (Map p138, B5; www.facebook.com/lavermubcn) A *vermuteria* with style: a marble bar; house-made *negre* (black) and *blanc* (white) vermouth; delicious fuss-free tapas such as cod croquettes.

La Vermuteria del Tano (Map p138, C3; www.facebook.com/ VermuteriaTano; Carrer de Joan Blanques 17) Scarcely changed in decades, with walls of barrels and marble-topped tables; the house-speciality Perucchi is served traditionally with a glass of carbonated water.

Vermuteria Puigmartí (Map p138, C4; Carrer de Puigmartí 12) A tiny, popular, brick-walled spot with a few tall street tables for savouring smoked sardines and homemade tortilla alongside house vermouth.

Bodega Marín (Map p138, D5; Carrer de Milà i Fontanals 72) A century-old classic given a new lease of life in 2022, Marín serves artisanal Reus-made vermouth, *cava* (sparkling wine) by the glass and traditional tapas (Cantabrian anchovies, Delta de l'Ebre oysters).

El Villa (Map p138, C5; www.elvillavermuteria.com; Carrer de Martínez de la Rosa 27) For a taste of Andalucía, pop into this nautical-feel *vermuteria del mar*, where Cádiz sherries and Catalan vermouths arrive with tapas of *fuet* (thin pork sausage) and smoked-fish *molletes* (soft bread rolls).

Drinking

Bobby Gin   COCKTAIL BAR

16 MAP P138, C5

With over 80 varieties, this whitewashed stone-walled bar mixes some of Barcelona's most artfully garnished goblet-sized G&Ts, courtesy of prize-winning bartender Alberto Pizarro. Try an infusion-based concoction such as citrus-infused Nordés, a cocktail like the L'Aperitiu Modernista (with cardamom bitters and the bar's own gin) or a signature Ginfonk, a cutting-edge cocktail-G&T fusion made with macerated gin. (www.bobbygin.com;)

SlowMov   COFFEE

17 MAP P138, B6

SlowMov founders Carmen and François work directly with coffee producers to responsibly source seasonal, single-origin beans, which are roasted on-site at their light-flooded Gràcia cafe with bar-style seating. With a keen sustainable focus (biodegradable packaging, deliveries by bike), this is one of Barcelona's original speciality coffee spots – and still one of the best. (www.slowmov.com; 📶)

14 de la Rosa

COCKTAIL BAR

18 🚇 MAP P138, C5

At this smart, intimate cocktail spot with vintage style (tiled floors, marble bar), subtly creative beauties are crafted by British mixologist Dean Shury. Or try the house vermouth, a natural Catalan wine or a Jerez sherry, with Km0 (local-ingredient) tapas (artisanal cheeses, local *fuet*). The Spanish Top Cocktail Bars awards named 14 de la Rosa one of Spain's three best in 2022. (www.14delarosa.com)

El Ciclista

COCKTAIL BAR

19 🚇 MAP P138, C5

As the name suggests, this elegant little cocktail bar is Barcelona's original cycle-themed boozy hang-out – expect bike-wheel chandeliers and tables, handlebar pieces and regular live music. G&Ts and flavoured mojitos shine on the cocktail list. (www.elciclistabar.com)

El Noa Noa

COFFEE

20 🚇 MAP P138, C4

A creative neighbourhood favourite, peach-toned Noa Noa is a speciality coffee spot that doubles as a small bookshop devoted to LGB-TIQ+, feminist, and art-and-design titles. Grab a flat white made with

Nømad (p89) beans and have a browse. (https://elnoanoa.es)

Elephanta

COCKTAIL BAR

21 🚇 MAP P138, C4

Off Gràcia's main drag, petite Elephanta has an old-fashioned feel, with plush green banquettes, art-lined walls and a five-seat bar with vintage stools. Gin is the drink of choice, with over 40 citrusy, botanical and classic dry options, including Catalan labels. (www.elephanta.cat; 📶)

Bar La Camila

BAR

22 🚇 MAP P138, D5

Everyday cafe-bar Camila has been reborn, keeping its traditional atmosphere (metal stools at the counter) while also bringing in a youthful creative touch (design magazines, plants in ceramic pots). Speciality coffee is sourced from top Spanish roasters, such as Valencia's female-founded Bluebell and Gràcia's own Slow-Mov, and there are natural wines, artisanal vermouths and local-produce tapas.

El Rabipelao

COCKTAIL BAR

23 🚇 MAP P138, C4

With DJs spinning salsa beats, occasional live music and a covered back patio, El Rabi is a celebratory space. Gins, Caribbean rums and tropical cocktails like mojitos and caipirinhas pair with Venezuelan-inspired vegan and vegetarian

Festa Major de Gràcia

During the popular week-long **Festa Major de Gràcia** (www.festamajordegracia.org), held around 15 August, local residents compete for the most elaborately decorated street. Free outdoor concerts, street fairs and other cultural events such as *correfocs* (fire runs) and *castells* (human towers) are all part of the fun. Most of the city's other districts host their own annual *festa*, including Poblenou, Sants, Barceloneta and Poble Sec.

tapas and *arepas* (filled cornbread patties). (www.elrabipelao.com)

Viblioteca   WINE BAR

24 🔒 MAP P138, B4

A glass cabinet piled high with ripe cheese (over 50 varieties), sourced from small-scale European producers, entices you into this small, white-walled, cleverly designed space. The real speciality at Viblioteca, however, is wine, and you can choose from 150 mostly local labels. (www.viblioteca.com)

Syra Coffee   COFFEE

25 🔒 MAP P138, C5

A loyal crowd of regulars queues up at check-floored Syra for takeaway flat whites, espressos and cappuccinos, brewed with seasonal, single-origin, sustainably produced beans roasted in Barcelona. Branches across the city. (http://syra.coffee)

Bar Salvatge   WINE BAR

26 🔒 MAP P138, B4

With its neon-lit ceiling logo and wine-festival posters, Salvatge specialises in (sensibly priced) natural wines both on tap and from the bottle, including plenty of Catalan labels and even a local vermouth. Perfect with the smoked-burrata quesadillas, tomato-and-cherry salads or artisanal cheeses. (https://barsalvatge.com)

Châtelet   COCKTAIL BAR

27 🔒 MAP P138, C4

A popular Gràcia meeting point, Châtelet has big windows, excellent cocktails and a buzzing, art-filled interior with decorative surfboards, ever-changing exhibitions and old-school American soul in the background.

Entertainment

Soda Acústic   LIVE MUSIC

28 ⭐ MAP P138, B4

One of Gràcia's most innovative performance spaces, this low-lit modern venue stages an eclectic collection of bands, artists and jams: jazz, world music, Balkan swing, Latin rhythms and plenty of experimental, not-easily-classifiable musicians. (www.soda.cat)

Shopping

Casa Atlàntica
CERAMICS

29 🔒 MAP P138, C5

The beautiful basketry and custom-designed bowls, mugs, plant pots, vases and other ceramics dotting this charming studio-boutique are collected by Galician artisans Belén and Lester, who collaborate with small-scale, family-owned village workshops across Galicia and Portugal to keep traditional crafts alive. Their work graces popular venues around town, as well as New York's MoMA. (www.casaatlantica.es)

Fromagerie Can Luc
CHEESE

30 🔒 MAP P138, A5

At any given time, this inviting shop stocks 150 different varieties of European cheese; Catalan favourites are the speciality, though you'll spot choices from France, Italy, the Netherlands, Switzerland, Britain and beyond. Wines, condiments, crackers and cheese knives are available too, along with gourmet picnic hampers and tasting sets. (www.canluc.es)

Mercat de l'Abaceria Central
MARKET

31 🔒 MAP P138, D4

An atmospheric neighbourhood market for stocking up on fresh produce, cheeses, charcuterie and Catalan meals to go, or grabbing a quick bite on the cheap. Stallholders were relocated to this site on Passeig de Sant Joan in 2019, while the original 1892 iron-and-brick market on Travessera de Gràcia undergoes restorations (though works were on hold indefinitely at the time of writing). (www.mercatabaceria.cat)

Bodega Bonavista
WINE

32 🔒 MAP P138, C6

An excellent little neighbourhood bodega-and-deli, Bonavista seeks

Ecofriendly Boutiques

Olokuti (Map p138, B4; https://olokuti.com; Carrer d'Astúries 38) From organic-cotton dresses to beautiful recycled-paper notebooks, every tempting item at this pioneering eco-boutique is both sustainable and fair trade.

Green Life Style (Map p138, C5; www.greenlifestyle.es; Carrer del Torrent de l'Olla 95) All-organic, sustainable fashion by independent European designers, with a focus on minimal capsule-style collections and a timeless feel.

Velvet BCN (Map p138, B3; www.velvetbcn.com; Carrer de Verdi 42) It's all about local brands, organic fabrics and fair-trade fashion at Velvet (stylish dresses, ceramic earrings, zero-waste beauty products).

Revolution Vintage (Map p138, B3; Carrer de Verdi 80) A preloved paradise of denim jackets, Levi's jeans and Hawaiian shirts.

out great wines at reasonable prices, mostly from Catalonia, elsewhere in Spain, and France. You can sample wines by the glass, along with cheeses and charcuterie, at the in-store tables.

Amalia Vermell JEWELLERY

33 MAP P138, B5

Striking geometric jewellery made from high-quality materials such as sterling silver is hand-crafted right here in the atelier by designer-owner Pamela Masferrer. Browse for pendants, necklaces, bracelets and rings, as well as vibrant homeware pieces and dresses by Barcelona brands. (www.amaliavermell.com)

Hibernian BOOKS

34 MAP P138, B4

Barcelona's only secondhand English bookshop stocks tens of thousands of titles covering all sorts of subjects, from cookery to romance to children's classics, plus a few new titles. (www.hibernianbooks.com)

Mushi Mushi FASHION & ACCESSORIES

35 MAP P138, C6

A gorgeous little boutique in an area that's not short of them, Mushi Mushi specialises in elegant women's fashion and accessories, highlighting small independent labels such as Des Petits Hauts, Sessùn and Soeur. (www.mushimushicollection.com)

View from Bunkers del Carmel (p141)

NOPPASIN WONGCHUM/GETTY IMAGES ©

The Changing Fortunes of Catalonia

Catalan identity is a multifaceted phenomenon, but Catalans are, more than anything else, united by the collective triumphs and shared grievances of the region's tumultuous past.

The Catalan golden age began in the early 12th century when Ramon Berenguer III, who already controlled Catalonia and parts of southern France, launched the region's first seagoing fleet. In 1137, his successor, Ramon Berenguer IV, was betrothed to Petronila, the one-year-old heiress to the Aragonese throne, thereby giving Catalonia sufficient power to expand its empire out into the Mediterranean. By the end of the 13th century, Catalan rule extended to the Balearic Islands and Catalonia's seaborne trade brought riches.

But weakened by a decline in trade and foreign battles, Catalonia became vulnerable. And when Fernando became king of Aragón in 1479 and married Isabel, Queen of Castile, Catalonia became a province of Castile. Catalonia resented its new subordinate status but could do little to overturn it. After backing the losing side in the War of the Spanish Succession (1702–13), Barcelona rose up against the Spanish crown, whose armies besieged the city from March 1713 until 11 September 1714. The victorious Felipe V abolished Catalan self-rule, built a huge fort (the Ciutadella) to watch over the city, banned writing and teaching in the Catalan language, and farmed out Catalonia's colonies to other European powers.

Trade again flourished from Barcelona in the following centuries, and by the late 19th and early 20th centuries there were growing calls for greater self-governance to go with the city's burgeoning economic power. However, after Spanish general Francisco Franco's civil war victory in 1939, Catalan Francoists and the dictator's army shot, in purges, at least 35,000 people, most of whom were anti-Franco or presumed to be so. Over time, the use of Catalan in public was banned, all street and town names were changed into Spanish, and Castilian Spanish was the only permitted language in schools and the media. Franco's lieutenants remained in control of the city until his death in 1975, and the sense of grievance remains – though today it's directed against the central government in Madrid.

Following an unsuccessful attempt by Catalonia to declare independence in 2017 (which saw nine separatist Catalan leaders jailed in 2019, then officially pardoned in 2021), the region's drive for autonomy still simmers, though local opinion remains split.

Camp Nou, Pedralbes & La Zona Alta

Some of Barcelona's most sacred sights are situated within the huge expanse stretching northwest beyond L'Eixample: the monastery of Pedralbes and the great shrine to Catalan football, Camp Nou. Other reasons to venture here are Tibidabo hill, the trails of the Parc Natural de Collserola, the thriving dining scene and the untouristed former towns of Sarrià and Sant Gervasi.

The Short List

○ **Reial Monestir de Santa Maria de Pedralbes (p153)** *Wandering the 14th-century cloister and admiring exquisite medieval murals.*

○ **Parc Natural de Collserola (p153)** *Escaping into the pine-forested hills for hiking, cycling and running.*

○ **Bellesguard (p153)** *Gazing upon Gaudí's medieval-style masterpiece, then strolling down to Sarrià.*

○ **CosmoCaixa (p153)** *Travelling through Earth's evolution at this excellent science museum.*

○ **Camp Nou (p155)** *Cheering along at a FC Barcelona game or reliving the team's great moments with a tour.*

Getting There & Around

Ⓜ Línia 3 for Camp Nou and Palau de Pedralbes (Palau Reial).

🚃 FGC trains for Tibidabo and the Parc Natural de Collserola.

🚋 A funicular runs to Tibidabo from Plaça del Doctor Andreu (reached by shuttle bus).

Neighbourhood Map on p152

Church and view from Tibidabo hill (p153) VUNAV/SHUTTERSTOCK ©

Tibidabo

Parc Natural de Collserola

Plaça del Doctor Andreu

Tram route temporarily closed for restoration

CosmoCaixa

For reviews see
⊙	Sights	p153
✕	Eating	p155
🍷	Drinking	p157

Ronda de Dalt

Ronda de Dalt

Av del Tibidabo

Vallcarca

ABaC

Av Tibidabo

Jardins del Turó del Putxet

Peu del Funicular

Av de Vallvidrera

Bellesguard

C d'Ivader

C d'Anglí

Pg de la Bonanova

C de Mandri

C de Ganduxer

C de les Escoles Pies

Ronda del General Mitre

C de Muntaner

C de Santaló

Pàdua

GRÀCIA

Lesseps

C de Saragossa

SANT GERVASI

Molina

Sant Gervasi

Reina Elisenda

Plaça de Sarrià

Sarrià

Les Tres Torres

La Bonanova

Muntaner

Gràcia

Parc de l'Oreneta

C del Bisbe Català

SARRIÀ

C Major de Sarrià

Via Augusta

Mercat de Galvany

Parc del Turó

Hisop

Travessera de Gràcia

Reial Monestir de Santa Maria de Pedralbes

Pg de Sant Joan Bosco

Av de Josep Vicenç Foix

Vil·la Amèlia Garden

Plaça de la Reina Maria Cristina

Av de Pau Casals

Av de Sarrià

Plaça de Francesc Macià

C del Comte d'Urgell

C de Paris

PEDRALBES

Pavellons Güell

Jardins del Palau de Pedralbes

Av de Pedralbes

Maria Cristina

Gran Via de Carles III

Av Diagonal

Cocina Hermanos Torres

C d'Entença

C de Viladomat

Hospital Clínic

Palau Reial

ZONA UNIVERSITÀRIA

Av de Joan XXIII

LES CORTS

C de Numància

Av de Josep Tarradellas

Entença

Av de Roma

NOVA ESQUERRA DE L'EIXAMPLE

Barça Stadium Tour & Museum

Camp Nou

Les Corts

Plaça del Centre

C de Berlín

Sants Estació

Tarragona

Parc de Joan Miró

C d'Arístides Maillol

SANTS

Estació Sants

C de Tarragona

Ctra de Collblanc

Travessera de Les Corts

Av de Madrid

Badal

Plaça de Sants

Parc de l'Espanya Industrial

Hostafrancs

Espanya

Collblanc

LA TORRASSA

Mercat de Sants

C de Sants

C de la Creu Coberta

Sights

Reial Monestir de Santa Maria de Pedralbes

CONVENT

1 MAP P152, A4

Founded in 1327, Pedralbes' serene convent is now a museum of monastic life (the few remaining nuns live nearby). It stands in a peaceful residential area that was countryside until the 20th century. The convent's architectural highlight is the large, elegant, three-storey cloister, a jewel of Catalan Gothic, built in the early 14th century. The sober church is another excellent example of Catalan Gothic. (http://monestirpedralbes.bcn.cat)

Parc Natural de Collserola

PARK

2 MAP P152, A1

Barcelonins often escape to this protected, pine-scented 83-sq-km park on the northwest edge of the city, with sprawling urban views. It's a great place to hike, run and bike (the 10km Carretera de les Aigües is a popular route), and has a smattering of country chapels (some Romanesque), the Tibidabo sights and the ruined 14th-century Castellciuro castle. The park information centre is at Carretera de l'Església 92 (near Baixador de Vallvidrera FGC station). (www.parcnaturalcollserola.cat)

CosmoCaixa

MUSEUM

3 MAP P152, B2

One of the city's most popular family-friendly attractions, this museum covers many fascinating areas of science, from fossils to physics to outer space. The highlight is the re-creation of more than 1 sq km of flooded Amazon rainforest (*Bosc Inundat*); over 100 species of Amazon flora and fauna (including anacondas, poisonous frogs and capybaras) live in this unique, living diorama in which you can even experience a tropical downpour. (Museu de la Ciència; www.cosmocaixa.com)

Tibidabo

MOUNTAIN

4 MAP P152, A1

Framing the north end of the city, the pine-forested mountain of Tibidabo (512m) is the highest peak in the beautifully green Serra de Collserola. Highlights include superb views; an old-fashioned **amusement park** (www.tibidabo.cat;); a **telecommunications tower** (www.torredecollserola.com); and a looming 20th-century **church** (https://tibidabo.salesianos.edu) by Enric Sagnier. The **Cuca de Llum** funicular runs to the top from Plaça del Doctor Andreu.

Bellesguard

ARCHITECTURE

5 MAP P152, B2

An entrancing work that combines Gothic and Modernista elements, this lesser-known, now-restored

Gaudí masterpiece was built between 1900 and 1909. Still owned by the Guilera family, the private residence has a castle-like appearance with crenellated walls of stone and brick, narrow stained-glass windows, elaborate ironwork, gorgeous gardens and a turret topped by a colourfully tiled Gaudían cross, along with spectacular city views. There's been a manor here since the 1400s. (www.bellesguardgaudi.com)

Mercat de Galvany   MARKET

6 ⊙ MAP P152, D4

Opened in 1927, Galvany is one of the city's most beautiful markets, with a red-brick facade, a soaring glass and cast-iron interior and over 80 stalls. The nearby

Parc del Turó (Avinguda de Pau Casals) is a peaceful green space with water lilies and its own cafe, **Pinhan** (www.pinhan.es;). (www.mercatgalvany.es)

Pavellons Güell   ARCHITECTURE

7 ⊙ MAP P152, A5

Created by Gaudí for the former Finca Güell, attached to today's **Palau de Pedralbes**, these stables and the porter's lodge were built between 1884 and 1887, when Gaudí was strongly impressed by Islamic architecture. Among the Palau's enchanting gardens, you'll also find a vine-covered parabolic pergola and a gurgling fountain of Hercules, both little-known Gaudí treasures. (www.portalgaudi.cat)

Reial Monestir de Santa Maria de Pedralbes (p153)

Making the Trip to Hallowed Camp Nou

A pilgrimage site for football fans from around the world, **Camp Nou** is a must for FC Barcelona fans. The stadium, built in 1957 and enlarged for the 1982 World Cup, is one of the world's biggest; once current renovations wrap up, it will have a capacity of 106,000 (there are 104,000 members). If you can't make a live game, the **Barça Stadium Tour** (Map p152, A6; www.fcbarcelona.com) offers an in-depth spin through the high-tech museum (delving into the club's history, its social commitment and connection to Catalan identity), followed by an exploration of the stadium itself.

Eating

Vivanda
CATALAN €€

8 MAP P152, A3

Diners are in for a treat with the knockout menu conceived by acclaimed Catalan chef Jordi Vilà, who also runs Sant Antoni's Alkímia (p171). Delicate tapas and *platillos* (sharing plates) showcase the freshest seasonal fare, from artisan cheeses and wild fish of the day to flamed aubergine with miso and orange. (www.vivanda.cat;)

Aspic
CAFE €€

9 MAP P152, C4

At the flagship cafe-deli of this high-end Barcelona caterer, luxury ingredients – smoked salmon, premium cheeses, high-grade olive oils – step into the spotlight in superb seasonal tapas, creative market-based salads and dishes like squid with *botifarra* (sausage) and Santa Pau beans. (www.aspic. es;)

La Balmesina
PIZZA €€

10 MAP P104, D4

For many *barcelonins*, this is the best pizza in town – La Balmesina was named one of the globe's greatest pizzerias in 2022 by 50 Top Pizza. Using organic flour and fresh, seasonal ingredients, its doughy delights are slow-fermented and topped with, for example, tomato, nduja, burrata and olives (the Calàbria). Italian owners Massimo and Alessandro also run nearby Gina Balmesina. (https://labalmesina.com)

Bambarol
TAPAS €€

11 MAP P152, D4

It's all about fresh, Mediterranean flavours at Santaló favourite Bambarol, led by chef Ferran Maicas, who has trained at some of Catalonia's top restaurants. On the short, seasonal menu, thoughtfully prepared traditional tapas such as Iberian-ham croquettes, *patates braves* and scallops with pork jowl mingle with creative global-influenced plates like fried chicken with kimchi mayonnaise. (https://bambarol.cat)

Tapas 24

TAPAS €

12 MAP P152, D4

Barcelona's beloved chef Carles Abellán brings his signature upmarket twist on classic tapas to this neon-lit corner cafe overlooking busy Diagonal – it's slightly quieter than its Eixample sibling (p126). Top picks are the sensational truffle and cured ham *bikini* (toastie), just-cooked tortilla, lemon-marinated anchovies and creamy Andalucian *payoyo* cheese. No bookings. (www.carlesabellan.com)

Michelin-Star Meals

Hisop (Map p152, D4; www.hisop.com) Catalan chef Oriol Ivern's Michelin-star venture, with artful seasonal menus.

Cocina Hermanos Torres (Map p152, C5; https://cocinahermanostorres.com) A reimagined tyre workshop in Les Corts hosts this three-Michelin-star venture.

ABaC (Map p152, C2; https://abacrestaurant.com) One of Barcelona's three triple-Michelin-star addresses, by Jordi Cruz.

Ultramarinos Marín

TAPAS €€

13 MAP P152, D4

Retaining the traditional charm of its everyday-bar predecessor, Ultramarinos Marín has become a hot favourite under well-known chef Borja García. Superb produce is at the heart of every deftly prepared bite on the misleadingly simple menu, from grilled *escalivada* (smoky grilled veggies), chicken or prawns to marinated fish of the day. (http://ultramarinosmarin.com)

Dalt de Tot

TAPAS €

14 MAP P152, D3

A fun local crowd gathers around the marble-top bar at this busy tapas-and-vermouth hang-out, just north of Sant Gervasi's Plaça Molina, for anchovies, house-made vermouth and tapas of Padrón peppers, cheeses, freshly cooked tortilla and Catalan-style *gildas*. (https://morrofi.cat)

Bangkok Cafe

THAI €€

15 MAP P152, C5

If you're craving authentically delicious Thai cuisine, Les Corts' buzzing, long-running Bangkok Cafe is just the ticket, with an open kitchen, photos of Thai royals and blackboard specials. It serves spicy green papaya salad, red curries, noodle stir-fries and other standouts. (www.facebook.com/bangkokcafebarcelona)

A Wander Through Old Sarrià

The old centre of elegant, affluent Sarrià is a largely pedestrianised haven of cosy squares, upmarket homes and slender streets. Founded in the 13th or 14th century, it was incorporated into Barcelona only in 1921 (the last surrounding town to be swallowed). Today's neighbourhood still centres on sinuous, sloping **Carrer Major de Sarrià**, with a sprinkling of shops and restaurants. At the street's top (north) end is pretty **Plaça de Sarrià**, overlooked by the 18th-century **Església de Sant Vicenç de Sarrià**, and with the 20th-century fresh-produce **Mercat de Sarrià** across the road. Buses 68 and V7 pass here.

As you wander downhill, duck into **Plaça del Consell de la Vila** and leafy **Plaça de Sant Vicenç de Sarrià**. Head south again to reach the 1902 **Portal Miralles** on Passeig de Manuel Girona – a little-visited, minor Gaudí creation. Top restaurants in Sarrià include **Bar Tomàs** (Map p152, B4; www.eltomasdesarria.com; Carrer Major de Sarrià 49), 1886-founded bakery **Foix de Sarrià** (Map p152, A3; www.foixdesarria.com; Plaça de Sarrià 12-13), vermouth-and-tapas spot **Morro Fi** (Map p152, B3; https://morrofi.cat; Passeig de la Bonanova 105) and Jordi Vilà's elegant **Vivanda** (p155).

Drinking

Gimlet
COCKTAIL BAR

16 MAP P152, D4

Under the watch of the talented team behind popular restaurant **Casa Fernández** next door, and Dry Martini (p128) in L'Eixample, red-dressed, stylishly updated Gimlet is one of Barcelona's oldest cocktail bars (though originally in a different location). Dry martinis and, of course, gimlets are the signature drinks. (www.drymartiniorg.com)

Oma Coffee
COFFEE

17 MAP P152, D4

The go-to friendly cafe for a strong brew near the Mercat de Galvany (p154), Oma serves stylish ceramic cups of velvety flat whites, double espresso and perfect cortados with beans from beloved El Born roaster El Magnífico (p91). (https://omabarcelona.com)

Mirablau
BAR

18 MAP P152, C1

Mirablau's balcony views over the entire city, from the base of the Tibidabo funicular, make up for sometimes patchy service. The bar-club is renowned for its impressive gin selection (including Galician Nordès and Catalonia's own Gin Mare) and has a dance space downstairs. (www.mirablaubcn.com)

Explore ⊚

Montjuïc, Poble Sec & Sant Antoni

Forested Montjuïc, the hillside overlooking the port, hosts some of the city's finest art collections, along with fragrant gardens, an imposing castle and fabulous views. Just below Montjuïc lie the lively tapas bars and leafy streets of Poble Sec, while the fashionable neighbourhood of Sant Antoni draws a stylish young crowd.

The Short List

○ **Museu Nacional d'Art de Catalunya (p160)** *Exploring six centuries of Catalan art, from Romanesque frescoes to relics from the Spanish Civil War.*

○ **Fundació Joan Miró (p162)** *Viewing brilliant works from one of the art world's giants, inside luminous galleries designed by Josep Lluís Sert.*

○ **Mercat de Sant Antoni (p168)** *Browsing this beautifully restored 19th-century market, before exploring the revitalised Sant Antoni neighbourhood.*

○ **Poble Sec food scene (p173)** *Cramming into heaving pintxo bars on Carrer de Blai and finding hidden-away tapas gems with a twist.*

○ **Outdoor Montjuïc (p164)** *Walking or running along pine-scented paths and in flower-filled gardens.*

Getting There & Around

Ⓜ Stops: Espanya, Poble Sec, Paral·lel, Sant Antoni.

🚌 Buses 150 and 55 serve Montjuïc.

🚡 Funicular from Paral·lel to Parc Montjuïc (part of the metro).

🚠 There are two cable cars up to Montjuic.

Neighbourhood Map on p166

Poble Espanyol (p168) CATARINA BELOVA/SHUTTERSTOCK ©

Top Experience 📷

Uncover Masterpieces at the Museu Nacional d'Art de Catalunya

The spectacular neobaroque silhouette of Montjuïc's Palau Nacional can be seen from across the city. Built for the 1929 World Exhibition and restored in 2005, the MNAC houses a vast collection of mostly Catalan art spanning the early Middle Ages to the 20th century. The highlights are the Romanesque frescoes and the insight the collection gives into the region's artistic progression.

◎ MAP P166, C4

www.museunacional.cat

Romanesque Masterpieces

Rescued from neglected country churches across northern Catalonia in the early 20th century, the Romanesque collection is considered the most important concentration of early medieval art in the world, and consists of 21 frescoes, woodcarvings and painted altar frontals. The insides of several churches have been recreated and the frescoes placed as they were when in situ. Most striking are the frescoes of the Virgin Mary and Christ, completed around 1123 in the nearby Església de Santa Maria de Taüll (Sala 9); the magnificent image of Christ in Majesty, completed around the same time and taken from the Eglésia de Sant Clement de Taüll (Sala 7); and the exceptional entryway from the 11th-century Església de Sant Joan de Boí (Sala 2).

Gothic Collection

Opposite the Romanesque collection, the Gothic art section has Catalan Gothic painting and works from other Spanish and Mediterranean regions. Keep an eye out especially for the work of Bernat Martorell in Sala 25 and Jaume Huguet in Sala 26.

Renaissance & Baroque

Next you pass into the Renaissance and Baroque gallery, which exhibits some 300 pieces, including works by Velázquez, Zurbarán, Ribera, Goya, Tiepolo, Rubens, El Greco and Canaletto.

Modern Catalan Art & the Spanish Civil War

The top floor's modern art collection includes works by Dalí, Gaudí, Picasso, Tàpies, Rusiñol and Fortuny, as well as the 2021-launched Spanish Civil War section (Sala 76 to Sala 80), which displays over 100 hard-hitting pieces that shine a light on this dark period, particularly poster art, painting and photojournalism.

★ Top Tips

○ Save money by purchasing the Articket BCN (https://articketbcn.org), a €35 pass to six museums (including the MNAC).

○ Be sure to take in the fine city view from the terrace just in front of the museum.

○ If you'd just like to see the building itself, there's a €2 entrance fee, which includes the view-laden roof terrace.

✕ Take a Break

There's a casual cafe on the museum's main level, and the elegant on-site restaurant **Òleum** (www.museunacional.cat) serves a seasonal Mediterranean *menú*.

Alternatively, wander 10 minutes down into Poble Sec to Barcelona's favourite Italian restaurant, Xemei (p171).

Top Experience 📷
Wander into Miró's Imagination at the Fundació Joan Miró

Joan Miró, the city's best-known 20th-century artistic progeny, bequeathed this art foundation to his home town in 1971. The gallery, designed by close friend and architect Josep Lluís Sert (who also built Miró's studios), is considered one of the world's most outstanding museum buildings and is crammed with seminal works, from Miró's earliest sketches to paintings from his last years.

◎ MAP P166, E4

www.fmirobcn.org

Sert's Temple to Miró's Art

Architect Josep Lluís Sert designed the shimmering white temple to one of Spain's artistic luminaries. The foundation rests amid the Montjuïc greenery and holds the greatest single collection of Miró's work, including around 220 of his paintings, 180 sculptures, some textiles and more than 8000 drawings spanning his entire life. Only a small portion is ever on display, interspersed with courtyards, water features and olive trees.

Early Years

The permanent collection is spread across 12 rooms, with thoughtfully positioned exhibits giving a broad impression of Miró's artistic development. Sala 1 has a few early works (1912–19) demonstrating the young Miró's relatively naturalistic approach before he started to develop his own very individual styles, while Sala 2 exhibits pieces from the 1920s showing the emergence of symbolic shapes in his art.

Miró's Major Works

Sala 3 contains several masterworks from the 1960s and 1970s, including *Personatge davant del sol* (Figure in Front of the Sun; 1968; inspired by Japanese Buddhist symbology), *L'or de l'atzur* (The Gold of the Azure; 1967) and the triptych *L'Esperança del condemnat a mort* (The Hope of a Condemned Man), referencing the last execution of the Franco dictatorship, a Catalan anarchist called Salvador Puig Antich, in 1974.

Salas 5, 6 and 7 host works loaned from the Kazumasa Katsuta collection. Salas 8 and 9 show a selection from the 1930s to 1980s, including *Sobreteixim dels vuit paragües* (Patches with Eight Umbrellas), one of Miró's first ventures into textile art. Next up, Sala 11 holds *Tapís de la Fundació*, a giant tapestry in Miró's trademark primary colours.

★ Top Tips

o For the full experience, pay the extra €5 for the multimedia guide, which includes commentary on major works, additional info on Miro's life and work, and images and photographs.

o Don't miss the terrace with a great panorama of Barcelona forming the backdrop to Miró's sculpture *Lluna, sol i una estrella*.

o On the eastern side of the museum lies the Jardí de les Escultures, a small garden with modern sculptures.

✗ Take a Break

The light-flooded cafe-restaurant at the heart of the museum serves freshly prepared Mediterranean dishes; the courtyard is a fine spot for a drink.

A 500m walk east (head left when exiting), Salts Montjuïc (p165) has tapas, drinks, live music and fabulous city views.

Walking Tour 🚶

Montjuïc's Gardens & Panoramas

Looming above the port, sloping Montjuïc is best explored on foot along the numerous forest paths that zigzag through gardens and skirt the exciting sights. The key here is planning – there's far too much to see in one day! This itinerary takes in the area's finest viewpoints and green spaces, along routes beloved by runners, walkers and other barcelonins getting active on Montjuïc.

Walk Facts

Start Castell de Montjuïc (🚌150 or 🚠)

End Jardins de Joan Maragall; Av de l'Estadi–Pg Olímpic (🚌55)

Length 3km; 1½ hours

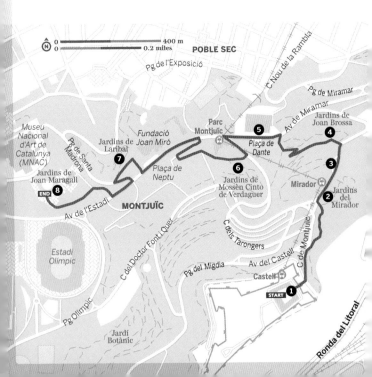

❶ Castell de Montjuïc

Take the Telefèric de Montjuïc cable car to the hilltop Castell de Montjuïc (p168); its dark history is today overshadowed by the stupendous views over Barcelona. Don't miss the sea-facing trail behind the fortress.

❷ Jardins del Mirador

A short stroll northeast down the shaded Camí del Mar pedestrian trail leads to another inspiring viewpoint over the city and sea at the palm-studded Jardins del Mirador, opposite the Mirador cable-car station.

❸ Plaça de la Sardana

Immediately downhill, Plaça de la Sardana is decorated with a sculpture of people dancing Catalonia's traditional folk dance, the *sardana*.

❹ Jardins de Joan Brossa

To the left of the square lie the charming landscaped Jardins de Joan Brossa, with fine panoramas from the site of a former amusement park, now covered in cypresses, cedars, pines, olive trees and large fan palms.

❺ Salts Montjuïc

Take a break with a view at all-day terrace tapas bar Salts Montjuïc (www.saltsmontjuic.com), overlooking Montjuïc's municipal pools; there's often live music to go with *patates braves*, squid-ink croquettes and other delicious tapas.

❻ Jardins de Mossèn Cinto de Verdaguer

Cross Carrer dels Tarongers to the painstakingly laid out Jardins de Mossèn Cinto de Verdaguer, home to 80,000 bulbs. Wander between tulips, narcissus, crocuses, varieties of dahlia, lotus flowers, water lilies and much more.

❼ Jardins de Laribal

Just beyond the Fundació Joan Miró, the soothing terraced gardens of the 1922-opened Jardins de Laribal are linked by paths, stairs and wisteria-clad walkways, with pretty sculpted watercourses inspired by Granada's Alhambra.

❽ Jardins de Joan Maragall

Continue 300m west to reach the little-visited Jardins de Joan Maragall (open Saturdays and Sundays from 10am to 3pm), with ornamental fountains and a neoclassical palace – the Spanish royal family's residence in Barcelona. Alternatively, head north out of the Jardins de Laribal to reach neighbouring Poble Sec, where tempting *pintxo* (Basque tapas) bars lie in wait.

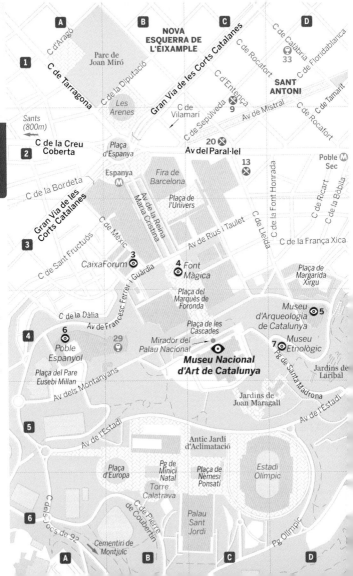

NOVA
ESQUERRA DE
L'EIXAMPLE

SANT
ANTONI

Poble M
Sec

A
B
C
D

1
2
3
4
5
6

C d'Aragó

Parc de
Joan Miró

C de Tarragona

C de la Diputació

Gran Via de les Corts Catalanes

C de Rocafort

C de Calàbria
33

C de Floridablanca

C d'Entença

Les
Arenes

C de
Vilamarí

C de Sepúlveda
9

Av de Mistral

C de Tamarit

C de Rocafort

Sants
(800m)

C de la Creu
Coberta

Plaça
d'Espanya

20
Av del Paral·lel

13

C de la Font Honrada

Espanya M

Fira de
Barcelona

Plaça de
l'Univers

C de Ricart

C de la Bòbila

C de la Bordeta

Gran Via de les
Corts Catalanes

C de Mèxic

Av de la Reina Maria Cristina

Av de Rius i Taulet

C de Lleida

C de la França Xica

C de Sant Fructuós

C de Francesc Ferrer i Guàrdia

CaixaForum 3

4 Font
Màgica

Plaça del
Marquès de
Foronda

Plaça de
Margarida
Xirgu

Museu
d'Arqueologia
de Catalunya 5

C de la Dàlia

Av de Francesc Ferrer i Guàrdia

6
Poble
Espanyol

29

Plaça de les
Cascades

Mirador del
Palau Nacional

Museu Nacional
d'Art de Catalunya

7 Museu
Etnològic

Pg de Santa Madrona

Jardins de
Laribal

Plaça del Pare
Eusebi Millan

Av dels Montanyans

Jardins de
Joan Maragall

Av de l'Estadi

Av de l'Estadi

Antic Jardí
d'Aclimatació

Estadi
Olímpic

C dels Jocs de 92

Plaça
d'Europa

C de Pierre de Coubertin

Pg de
Minici
Natal
Torre
Calatrava

Plaça de
Nèmesi
Ponsatí

Palau
Sant
Jordi

Pg Olímpic

Cementiri de
Montjuïc

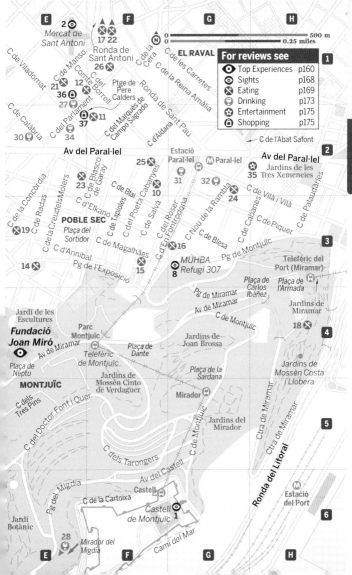

Montjuïc, Poble Sec & Sant Antoni

For reviews see

⦿	Top Experiences	p160
⦿	Sights	p168
⊗	Eating	p169
⊗	Drinking	p173
⊛	Entertainment	p175
ⓐ	Shopping	p175

EL RAVAL

0 ——— 500 m
0 ——— 0.25 miles

Mercat de Sant Antoni

Ronda de Sant Antoni

C de Viladomat
C de Manso
C del Comte Borrell
Ptge de Pere Calders
Ronda de Sant Pau
C de la Cera
C de les Carretes
C de la Reina Amàlia

C de Calàbria
C del Parlament
C del Marquès de Campo Sagrado
C d'Aldana

C de l'Abat Safont

Av del Paral·lel

Estació Paral·lel
Ⓜ Paral·lel

Jardins de les Tres Xemeneies

Av del Paral·lel

C de la Concòrdia
C de Radàs
C de la Creu dels Molers
C de Blasco de Garay
C de Blai
C de Tapioles
C del Poeta Cabanyes
C de Salvà
C d'Elkano
C del Roser
C d'En Fontrodona
C Nou de la Rambla
C de Blesa
C de Vilà i Vilà
C de Cabanes
C de Piquer
C de Palaudàries

POBLE SEC

Plaça del Sortidor

C de Magalhães
C d'Annibal

Pg de l'Exposició

Pg de Montjuïc

MUHBA Refugi 307

Teleféric del Port (Miramar)

Plaça de Carlos Ibáñez
Plaça de l'Armada

Jardins de Miramar

Pg de Miramar
Av de Miramar
C de Montjuïc

Jardí de les Escultures

Parc Montjuïc
Teleféric de Montjuïc

Plaça de Dante

Jardins de Joan Brossa

Fundació Joan Miró

Plaça de Neptú

MONTJUÏC

Av de Miramar

Jardins de Mossèn Cinto de Verdaguer

Plaça de la Sardana

Mirador

Jardins de Mossèn Costa i Llobera

C dels Tres Pins
C del Doctor Font i Quer

Jardins del Mirador

Ctra de Miramar

Ronda del Litoral

C dels Tarongers

Av del Castell

Castell

Castell de Montjuïc

C de la Cartoixa

Camí del Mar

Estació del Port

Pg del Migdia

Jardí Botànic

Mirador del Migdia

Sights

Castell de Montjuïc   FORTRESS

1 ◉ MAP P166, G6

Enjoying commanding views over the Mediterranean, Barcelona's forbidding fortress dominates the southeastern heights of Montjuïc. It dates from the late 17th and 18th centuries, though there's been a watchtower here since 1073. For most of its dark history, Montjuïc's castle has been a political prison and killing ground. Anarchists were executed here in the late 19th century, fascists during the civil war and Republicans after it – most notoriously Republican Catalan president Lluís Companys in 1940. (https://ajuntament.barcelona.cat)

Mercat de Sant Antoni   MARKET

2 ◉ MAP P166, E1

Sant Antoni's glorious iron-and-brick market was originally completed in 1882 by Catalan architect Antoni Rovira i Trias. Following a nine-year renovation job, it reopened with 250 stalls and several cafe-bars in 2018, kicking off a new buzz in the area. On Sundays, it hosts an open-air, 1937-founded **secondhand-book market** (www.mercatdominicaldesantantoni.com). (www.mercatdesantantoni.com)

CaixaForum   GALLERY

3 ◉ MAP P166, B3

La Caixa bank's premier Barcelona expo space hosts part of its extensive global art collection, as well as fascinating temporary international exhibitions, in the renovated Casaramona factory, an outstanding brick Modernista creation by Josep Puig i Cadafalch. (www.caixaforum.es)

Font Màgica   FOUNTAIN

4 ◉ MAP P166, B3

Originally created for the 1929 World Exposition, this huge colour-lit fountain has again been a magnet since the 1992 Olympics. Each evening, it bursts into a 15-minute musical, backlit display (repeated several times).

Museu d'Arqueologia de Catalunya   MUSEUM

5 ◉ MAP P166, D4

Occupying the 1929 World Exhibition's Graphic Arts Palace, Barcelona's intriguing archaeology museum covers both Catalonia and cultures from across Spain. There's good material on the Balearic Islands (including 5th- to 3rd-century BCE statues of Phoenician goddess Tanit from Ibiza) and the Greek and Roman city of Empúries. Don't miss the 53,200-year-old human jaw found near Sitges, or the beautiful Roman mosaic depicting Les Tres Gràcies (The Three Graces). (MAC; www.macbarcelona.cat)

Poble Espanyol   CULTURAL CENTRE

6 ◉ MAP P166, A4

Welcome to Spain! All of it! This 'Spanish Village' is an intriguing scrapbook of Spanish architecture, from Andalucía to Galicia, built for the local-crafts section of the 1929 World Exhibition. The 117 buildings include restaurants, cafes, bars, clubs (**La Terrazza**, p174), shops, artisanal workshops, and the **Fundació Fran Daurel** (www. fundaciofrandaurel.com) gallery (with Picasso, Miró and Barceló pieces). (www.poble-espanyol.com)

Museu Etnològic MUSEUM

7 ◉ MAP P166, D4

Delving into Catalonia's rich heritage, Barcelona's intriguing ethnology museum covers origin myths, religious festivals and folklore. There are several *gegants* (papier-mâché giants) and a dragon and devil costumes used in *correfocs* (fire runs). (www. barcelona.cat)

MUHBA Refugi 307 HISTORIC SITE

8 ◉ MAP P166, G3

Barcelona was the city most heavily bombed by Franco's air forces during the Spanish Civil War, and as a result it developed around 1300 air-raid shelters. Dug under a fold of northern Montjuïc by local citizens from 1937 to 1939, the 307th refuge is one of the city's best-preserved shelters, with over 400m of tunnels. Compulsory tours run on Sunday only (reservations essential). (http://ajuntament.barcelona.cat)

Eating

Enigma GASTRONOMY €€€

9 ⊗ MAP P166, C1

Celebrated chef Albert Adrià's Michelin-star galactic restaurant,

Castell de Montjuïc

GYPSYPICTURESHOW/SHUTTERSTOCK ©

Taking the Scenic Route with Barcelona's Cable Cars

The quickest and most scenic route from Barceloneta to Montjuïc mountain is aboard the **Telefèric del Port** (www.telefericodebarcelona. com; Passeig de Joan de Borbó) cable car, which runs between the Torre de Sant Sebastiá in Barceloneta and the Miramar stop on Montjuïc in seven minutes. From the Parc Montjuïc cable car station on northern Montjuïc, the separate **Telefèric de Montjuïc** (Map p166, F4; www.telefericdemontjuic.cat) whizzes you up to the **Castell de Montjuïc** (p168).

which resembles a 3D art installation, relaunched in mid-2022 with fresh 'fun dining'. Open only for lunch and afternoon drinks, it's a cutting-edge gastronomic journey with an easy-going twist – no tasting menu here, just a wildly creative seasonal menu of Adrià's favourite flavours, drawing on everything from sashimi to *entrepans* (filled rolls). (www. enigmaconcept.es)

Quimet i Quimet TAPAS €

10 MAP P166, F2

Now led by its fourth generation, family-run Quimet i Quimet has been passed down since 1914. There's barely space to swing a *calamar* (squid) in this bottle-lined, standing-room-only place popular with both *barcelonins* and visitors, but it's a treat for the palate. Try delectable made-to-order *montaditos* (tapas on bread), such as salmon with greek yoghurt and truffle honey, with one of the 500 wines. (www. quimetquimet.com)

Benzina ITALIAN €€

11 MAP P166, F2

A stylishly converted mechanic's garage sets the tone for Sant Antoni's favourite Italian restaurant, a New York-inspired hang-out where the vibe is lively, the cocktails expert-mixed and the food flawless. The menu changes every few months, and creative plates by chef Nicola Valle fuse local and Italian ingredients, such as the signature spaghetti carbonara. The switched-on team also runs *cicchetti* spot **Doppietta** (www. doppietta.es). (www.benzina.es;)

Federal CAFE €

12 MAP P166, E1

On Sant Antoni's main stretch, which now teems with cafes and boutiques, Australian-founded Federal was the trailbazer, with its expertly crafted coffee and superb creative brunches ranging from avocado toast with carrot hummus to baked eggs. Head to the breezy roof terrace or grab a cushioned window seat. (www.federalcafe.es; 🛜 ✈)

Casa de Tapas Cañota
TAPAS €€

13 🌐 MAP P166, C2

A friendly, family-owned old-timer, Cañota serves affordable, nicely turned out tapas. Seafood is the speciality, with rich razor clams, garlic-fried prawns and tender octopus. Wash it down with a refreshing bottle of *albariño* (a Galician white). (www.casadetapas.com)

Xemei
VENETIAN €€

14 🌐 MAP P166, E3

Everyone's favourite Italian, Xemei ('Twins' in Venetian) is a wonderful, authentically delicious slice of Venice in Barcelona, named for its twin Venetian owners Stefano and Max Colombo. To the accompaniment of gentle jazz and vintage-inspired design, you might try homemade pappardelle with ossobuco ragù *bigoli*, orange-and-cardamom risotto or fresh-pasta *cacio e pepe*. (www.xemei.es)

La Platilleria
TAPAS €

15 🌐 MAP P166, F3

Lovingly prepared tapas change depending on the day's seasonal produce at Argentine Fernando Silva's terrific tucked-away restaurant in upper Poble Sec. Tempting sharing plates rooted in traditional flavours, but with a light creative touch, might mean *patates braves*,

steak tartar, in-season calçots and *fricandó* (Catalan beef stew).

Palo Cortao
TAPAS €€

16 🌐 MAP P166, G3

Now relocated to the chic, contemporary **Hotel Brummell** (p179), welcoming Palo Cortao is renowned for its beautifully executed seafood and meat *raciones* with flavours of Andalucía, where its founders are from. Jerez sherry arrives alongside Cádiz-style *chicharrones*, fried aubergines with honey and miso, and Ebro Delta rice dishes. (www.palocortao.es)

Alkímia
CATALAN €€€

17 🌐 MAP P166, F1

Inside the innovatively redesigned 19th-century Fàbrica Moritz (p172) brewery, culinary alchemist Jordi Vilà creates refined Catalan dishes with a twist that have earned him a Michelin star. Wild fish of the day with chard, braised octopus in sea-style *menjablanc*, and artichoke stuffed with tuna-belly tartare are just a hint of the seasonal tasting menu. (www.alkimia.cat)

Martínez
SPANISH €€€

18 🌐 MAP P166, H4

With fabulous port panoramas and an open-late bar, stylish Martínez is a standout among Montjuïc's lacklustre dining scene. The terrace is ideal for warm-day lunches of the signature rice dishes, such as *arròs del senyoret*, along with market-fresh fish and grilled meats. (https://martinezbarcelona.com)

Casa Xica   FUSION €€

19 🍴 MAP P166, E3

A casual, artfully designed Poble Sec space where elements of various Asian cuisines are fused with fresh Catalan ingredients. Owners Marc and Raquel lived and travelled extensively in Asia, and their beautifully expressed dishes include Shanghai-style duck with noodles, catfish tacos and tiger's milk scallops. (https://casa-xica.es)

Iakni   MIDDLE EASTERN €€

20 🍴 MAP P166, C2

Lebanese-owned Iakni prepares glorious meze delights such as hummus, baba ganoush, muhammara, fattoush, falafel and halloumi, near Plaça d'Espanya. Everything is homemade, and there are Lebanese wines and fragrant mint teas. (www.iakni.com)

Maleducat   CATALAN €€

21 🍴 MAP P166, E1

Opposite Sant Antoni's market, popular Maleducat puts a con- temporary spin on the traditional Catalan casa de menjars (meals house). A raft of seasonal, market- fresh platillos (sharing plates) is its winning formula (slivers of Iberian ham, organic tomato salad), and the menu always includes a rice dish. (http://maleducat.es)

Fàbrica Moritz   GASTROPUB €€

22 🍴 MAP P166, F1

A 19th-century building dazzlingly remodelled by architect Jean Nouvel meets a menu by chef Jordi Vilà, of Michelin-starred Alkímia (p171) – also on the premises. The popular Moritz brewery-and- restaurant offers pan-European gastropub bites such as fish and chips and flammkuchen (Alsatian-style pizza), as well as Barcelona-style tapas. (http://fabricamoritzbarcelona.com)

Denassus   TAPAS

23 🍴 MAP P166, E2

Two respected sommeliers are behind this easy-going wine-and- tapas bar on Poble Sec's pintxo- packed Carrer de Blai, which sources most of its organic, natural drops from small, independent producers across Spain. Grab a table on the terrace for truffled tortillas, pulled-pork brioches and grilled leeks in citrus-and-agave sauce. (https://denassus.com)

Elche   SEAFOOD €€

24 🍴 MAP P166, G2

Old-world-style in service and setting, family-run Elche has been serving some of Barcelona's best rices and fideuà (paella-like noodle dish) since 1959. The arròs negre (squid-ink rice) with artichokes and the cod-and-mushroom rice are specialities. (www.elcherestaurant.es)

Carrer de Blai
Pintxo Bars

Carrer de Blai (Map p166, F2) in Poble Sec is packed with busy tapas and *pintxo* bars, where you can feast on bite-sized deliciousness at €1 to €2 a piece.

Blai 9 (https://blai9.com) Artfully prepared, creative *pintxos*, such as *pernil* (Iberian ham) on pancake and gooey tortilla.

Koska Taverna Locally loved little tavern for just-cooked tortilla with toppings, spiced *gildas* and more.

La Tasqueta de Blai (www.latasquetadeblai.com) Perfect *pintxos* with an innovative touch – grilled prawns in paper cones, fried squid in bread.

La Esquinita de Blai (www.facebook.com/laesquinitadeblai) Stop by this modern spot for herby prawn brochettes, stuffed *piquillo* peppers and meaty mini bao, with house vermouth.

La Chana   ANDALUCIAN €€

25 MAP P166, F2

A slice of sunny Andalucía in the thick of Poble Sec, La Chana celebrates all the best Cádiz-style tapas. It's a small, narrow space for devouring *pescaíto frito* (fried fish), Barbate *almadraba* tuna, vinegar-laced *papas aliñás* (potato salad) and a glass of *manzanilla* sherry. (www.facebook.com/lachanapoblesec)

Els Sortidors del Parlament   TAPAS €

26 MAP P166, F1

A rustic yet modern space filled with barrel tables, concrete floors and open-stone walls, this former motorbike workshop on Sant Antoni's trendiest street is popular for its house vermouth, Catalan wines and fuss-free *raciones*.

Drinking

Bar Calders   BAR

27 MAP P166, E1

A neighbourhood fave, Bar Calders is unbeatable as an all-day cafe, tapas, wine and vermouth bar, and its outdoor tables are go-to meeting points for Sant Antoni's boho crowd.

La Caseta del Migdia   BAR

28 MAP P166, E6

The effort of getting to what is, for all intents and purposes, a simple *xiringuito* (summer snack bar) perched atop Montjuïc's seaward slopes, is worth it. Gaze out on the Mediterranean over a beer or soft drink by day. Reggae, samba and funk waft out over the hillside as sunset approaches. (www.lacaseta.org)

La Terrrazza
CLUB

29 📍 MAP P166, B4

In warmer months, this re-created Balearic-style mansion attracts squadrons of locals and visitors for a full-on night of music (mainly house, techno and electronica), dancing, cocktails and vaguely Ibizan vibes. It's set partly under the stars, inside the Poble Espanyol (p168) complex. (http://laterrrazza.com;)

La Mari Ollero
WINE BAR

30 📍 MAP P166, E2

Dressed with red-brick walls and marble tables, elegant La Mari Ollero brings a cheery Andalucian touch to the classic Catalan *vermuteria*. Wines come from the south (including sherry-style Montilla-Moriles) as well as Catalonia and elsewhere in northern Spain. Tapas combine flavours from Barcelona and Córdoba, including *patates braves*, *salmorejo* (cold, tomato-based soup) and *cordobés* cheeses. (www.lamariollero.com)

La Federica
BAR

31 📍 MAP P166, G2

With drag shows, weekend parties, flamenco performances, rotating art exhibits and vintage decor, Poble Sec's La Federica is

Exploring Down-to-Earth Sants

Wedged between Plaça d'Espanya and Camp Nou, the little-touristed working-class neighbourhood of Sants was one of Barcelona's major 19th-century industrial hubs, dedicated mostly to producing textiles. Originally an independent town, it became part of Barcelona city in 1884, and today it retains its down-to-earth *barri* feel.

Wander along the leafy, elevated **Rambla de Sants** to reach the beautifully restored red-brick **Mercat de Sants** (Map p152, C6; https://mercatdesants.cat); first opened in 1913, it has a soaring interior crammed with fresh produce. Other neighbourhood highlights include tree-shaded **Plaça d'Osca**, lined with tapas-and-vermouth bars like Vermut i a la Gàbia, and the playfully postmodern **Parc de l'Espanya Industrial** (Map p152, C6). You'll find classic tapas at **Bodega Montferry** (Passatge de Serra i Arola 13), speciality coffee at zero-waste cafe **NEØ** (www.neocoffeehouse.com; Carrer Olzinelles 29), a gourmet vermouth-and-tapas scene at **La Mundana** (www.lamundana.cat), creative *menús* at Slow Food **Olivos Comida y Vinos** (www.olivoscomidayvinos.com; Carrer de Galileu 159), and upscale Japanese cooking at sky-high **Nobu** (https://barcelona.nobuhotels.com; Avinguda de Roma 2-4; ❄ 🛜). A great way to dive into Sants is on an expert-led food tour with **Culinary Backstreets** (p28).

a favourite of the local LGBTIQ+ scene. Thoughtfully prepared artisan tapas accompany well-mixed G&Ts, creative cocktails and Spanish wines. (www.facebook.com/barlafederica)

Abirradero
MICROBREWERY

32 🚇 MAP P166, G2

One of Barcelona's finest craft breweries has 40 of its own beers rotating on the taps, including IPAral·lel (a double IPA) and Trigotopia. Tapas, sharing boards and burgers are standouts from the kitchen, and you'll occasionally catch live music and brewery tours. (www.abirradero.com; 📶)

Garage Bar
WINE BAR

33 🚇 MAP P166, D1

The organisers of Barcelona's Vella Terra natural-wine festival have their own popular bar, shop and tapas spot on the Sant Antoni scene, stocking 150 world-roaming natural labels. The elegant local-produce menu keeps things creative, with burrata-and-fig salad, organic-cheese boards and rich *mojama* (salt-cured tuna). (https://garagebar.cat)

Cafè Cometa
COFFEE

34 🚇 MAP P166, E2

A cosy cafe with mismatched furniture, Cometa does perfect speciality coffee using beans from Barcelona roasters (such as Orbita Coffee), along with home-baked cakes and artisanal sandwiches. It also runs Cosmo (p129) in L'Eixample. (http://cafecometa.com; 📶)

Entertainment

Sala Apolo
LIVE MUSIC

35 ⭐ MAP P166, H2

Red velvet dominates, and you feel as though you're in a movie-set dancehall scene at this fine old theatre turned club and concert hall. Everything from local bands and burlesque shows to big-name international acts fuel diehard, never-stop-dancing nights. (www.sala-apolo.com)

Shopping

Llibreria Calders
BOOKS

36 🔒 MAP P166, E1

Spread across what was once a button factory, this lively bookshop and literary hub stocks both secondhand and brand-new titles in a stylish concrete-covered space. It emphasises local authors. (www.llibreriacalders.com)

Trait
FASHION & ACCESSORIES

37 🔒 MAP P166, E2

Spread across two concept boutiques on Sant Antoni's main boulevard, Trait has a thoughtfully curated collection of men's and women's fashion, minimal homewares and other trinkets. Browse through vegan Veja shoes, Rains backpacks, koi-shaped jugs, organic Meraki soaps and bold Hay vases. (https://traitstore.com)

Survival Guide

Castell (p67) MICH SEIXAS/500PX ©

Before You Go

Book Your Stay

o Wherever (and when-ever) you stay, book well ahead.

o Staying in the Barri Gòtic, El Raval or La Ribera puts you in the heart of the action, but nights can be noisy from Thursday to Sunday.

o L'Eixample can be quieter (assuming you're not on a busy boulevard), while Barceloneta and El Poblenou are perfect for the beach. Gràcia is popular for its village feel.

o Outer neighbourhoods mean more transport, but a quieter escape.

Useful Websites

Booking.com and, controversially, Airbnb are popular booking portals. Other options:

Aparteasy (www. aparteasy.com)

Apartment Barcelona (www. apartmentbarcelona. com)

Destination BCN (www. destinationbcn.com)

Barcelona

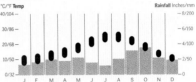

When to Go

o **Summer (Jun–Aug)** Hot beach weather and festival season, but of-ten overwhelmed with visitors; locals escape in August.

o **Autumn (Sep–Nov)** September is a top month to visit (includ-ing the Festes de la Mercé); October and November are quieter.

o **Winter (Dec–Feb)** Nights can be chilly and there's a chance of rain, but there are fewer visitors, plenty of sunny days and even seaside restaurants open.

o **Spring (Mar–May)** A lovely time to visit. Manageable visitor numbers; mixed weather.

Friendly Rentals (www. friendlyrentals.com)

Idealista (www. idealista.com)

Lonely Planet (www. lonelyplanet.com/ spain/barcelona/hotels)

MH Apartments (www. mhapartments.com)

Sonder (www. sonder.com)

Ukio (https://ukio.com)

Best Budget

Casa Gràcia (www.casagraciabcn. com) Stylish hostel with white-and-gold rooms.

360 Hostel Arts & Culture (www.360hostel.com) Buzzy scene in an art-filled design hostel.

Pensió 2000 (www. pensio2000.com) Family-run guesthouse overlooking the Palau de la Música Catalana.

Pars Tailor's Hostel (www.parshostels.com) Budget-chic Sant Antoni choice with vintage vibe.

Casa Jam (www. casajambarcelona. com) Forward-thinking Gràcia hostel/guest-house focused on sustainable tourism.

TOC Hostel (www.tochostels.com) Modern dorms, private rooms, dip pool; in L'Eixample.

Best Midrange

Praktik Rambla (www.hotelpraktikrambla.com) A 19th-century L'Eixample mansion turned boutique beauty; several other branches.

Hotel Brummell (www.hotelbrummell.com) Boutique bliss (pool, cafe, yoga) in Poble Sec.

Five Rooms (www.the5rooms.com) Charming L'Eixample pick with designer rooms.

Casa Mathilda (www.casamathilda.com) Intimate, styled-up 1920s building in northern L'Eixample.

Hotel Market (www.hotelmarketbarcelona.com) Stylish rooms in Sant Antoni.

Hostal Grau (www.hostalgrau.com) A 19th-century Raval *hostal* reborn with environmental awareness.

Best Top End

Casa Bonay (www.casabonay.com) Designer Catalan-inspired interiors in an 1896 L'Eixample building.

El Palace (www.hotelpalacebarcelona.com) A plushly updated grand dame of L'Eixample.

Hotel Neri (www.hotelneri.com) Beautiful, historical hotel in the thick of the Barri Gòtic.

Serras (www.hoteltheserrasbarcelona.com) Sleek portside five-star; rooftop pool.

Hotel Arts Barcelona (www.hotelartsbarcelona.com) Glossy design; awe-inspiring architecture.

Arriving in Barcelona

Aeroport de Barcelona–El Prat

The **Aeroport de Barcelona–El Prat** (www.aena.es; 🛜) lies 15km southwest of Plaça de Catalunya at El Prat de Llobregat.

○ Bus The **Aerobús** (https://aerobusbarcelona.es) runs between the airport and Plaça de Catalunya (30 to 40 minutes) via Plaça d'Espanya, Gran

Apartments & Overtourism

While private apartments might seem a convenient and cost-effective accommodation choice, it's important to know that Airbnb and other apartment rental agencies have been accused of contributing to Barcelona's overtourism problem and driving up prices (not to mention noise levels). The Barri Gòtic, El Raval, La Barceloneta and El Born have been particularly affected. Barcelona's authorities stopped issuing new licences in 2014 and since 2016 have been closing down unlicensed properties. By staying in a hotel (particularly an independent one), you support local businesses and workers (and even more so if you time your visit for low season). If booking an apartment, check first whether it's licensed at www.fairtourism.barcelona.

Via de les Corts Catalanes (corner of Carrer del Comte d'Urgell) and Plaça de la Universitat, with frequent services 24 hours a day. Buses from Plaça de Catalunya to the airport stop at the corner of Carrer de Sepúlveda and Carrer del Comte d'Urgell, and at Plaça d'Espanya (but not at Plaça de la Universitat). Route A1 serves Terminal 1, and Route 2 serves Terminal 2. The Plaça de Catalunya bus stop is on the east side of the square, outside El Corte Inglés. Fares on both are €5.90/10.20 single/return.

○ **Metro** *Línia* 9 Sud (L9S) connects T1 and T2 with Zona Universitària (32 minutes) every seven minutes 5am to midnight Sunday to Thursday, 5am to 2am on Friday and 24 hours on Sunday; change lines en route for Barcelona city centre (€5.15).

○ **Taxi** The cost is around €30 to/from the centre (30 minutes).

○ **Train** From around 5.30am to 11.30pm, Renfe (www.renfe.com) runs the half-hourly R2 Nord train line, linking the airport via several stops to Barcelona's main train station, Estació Sants (20 minutes), and to Passeig de Gràcia (27 minutes). If you need to change terminals to reach the airport train station, free 24-hour shuttle buses (allow 10 to 20 minutes) link T2 with T1 every five to 10 minutes.

Aeroport de Girona–Costa Brava

○ **Girona–Costa Brava airport** (www.aena.es), 13km southwest of Girona and 92km northeast of Barcelona, is served by flights from across Europe.

○ The **Sagalés Airport Line** (www.sagalesairportline.com) runs several times daily between Girona–Costa Brava airport and Barcelona's Estació del Nord bus station (€19.50, 1¼ hours).

Aeroport de Reus

○ **Reus airport** (www.aena.es), 13km west of Tarragona and 108km southwest of Barcelona, has flights from Europe.

○ **Monbus** (www.monbus.es) links Reus airport with Barcelona's Estació d'Autobusos de Sants (€16, 1¾ hours).

Estació Sants

○ Barcelona's main train station is Sants, 2.5km west of the Barri Gòtic.

○ Train is the most convenient and environmentally friendly option for reaching Barcelona from major Spanish centres like Madrid, Valencia and Seville. The high-speed TGV train takes around 6½ hours to/from Paris.

○ A network of *rodalies* (local trains) run by Renfe (www.renfe.com) serves towns around Barcelona (and the airport).

Estació d'Autobusos Barcelona Nord

○ Barcelona's long-haul **bus station** (https://barcelonanord.barcelona) is in L'Eixample, 1.5km northeast of Plaça de Catalunya and a short walk from the Arc de Triomf metro station. Buses fan out across Spain, many operated by **Alsa** (www.alsa.es).

○ International buses, including **Eurolines** (www.eurolines.de), serve Europe and Morocco from the Estació del Nord and the **Estació d'Autobusos de Sants**.

Getting Around

Metro

o The easy-to-use Transports Metropolitans de Barcelona (TMB) metro system (www.tmb.cat) has 11 numbered and colour-coded lines. It runs 5am to midnight Sunday to Thursday, to 2am on Friday and 24 hours on Saturday.

o The metro, FGC trains, *rodalies/cercanías* (Renfe-run local trains) and buses come under a combined system. Targeta T-Casual (10-ride passes; €11.35) are the best value and allow you to travel on different modes of transport; otherwise, it's €2.40 per ride in Zone 1.

Bus

o **Transports Metropolitans de Barcelona** (www.tmb.cat) buses run along most city routes every few minutes from between 5am and 6.30am to around 10pm and 11pm.

o After 11pm, **Nitbus** (www.ambmobilitat.cat) runs a reduced network of 20 night buses until 3am or 5am (including N17 to/from the airport). Many *nitbus* routes pass through Plaça de Catalunya and most run every 15 to 30 minutes.

Taxi

o Taxis charge €2.30 flag fall plus meter charges of €1.21 per kilometre (€1.45 from 8pm to 8am and all day on weekends). A further €4.30 is added for all trips to/from the airport and €2.50/€4.30 for journeys starting from Estació Sants/the port. You can flag a taxi down, call one or book through a wealth of app-and/or website-based companies, including **Taxi Ecològic** (http://taxiecologic.com) for electric vehicles.

Train

o Suburban trains, run by the **Ferrocarrils de la Generalitat de Catalunya** (FGC; www.fgc.cat), include useful city lines. All lines heading north from Plaça de Catalunya stop at Carrer de Provença and Gràcia; L7 goes to near Tibidabo and L6 goes to Sarrià and Reina Elisenda, near the Monestir de Pedralbes.

o FGC trains run from about 5am (with only one or two services before 6am) to 11pm or midnight Sunday to Thursday, and from 5am to about 1am on Friday and Saturday.

Bicycle

o Barcelona has over 200km of bike lanes, with more due for completion throughout 2023 – it's a very bike-friendly city.

o Bike-hire outlets are everywhere, particularly in the Barri Gòtic, El Raval and La Ribera; from €5 per hour.

o Barcelona's main bike-share scheme **Bicing** (www.bicing.barcelona) is geared towards residents rather than tourists.

Cable Car

o **Telefèric del Port** (www.telefericodebarcelona.com) Travels between the waterfront southwest of Barceloneta and Montjuïc.

o **Telefèric de Montjuïc** (Map p166; www.telefericdemontjuic.cat) Runs between Parc Montjuïc and the Castell de Montjuïc.

Essential Information

Accessible Travel

o All buses in Barcelona are wheelchair accessible, as are most metro stations (generally by lift, though there have been complaints that these are only good for people with prams; check www.tmb.cat/en/transport-accessible), hotels, street crossings and public institutions.

o Ticket-vending machines in metro stations are adapted for travellers with disabilities and have Braille options.

o **Barcelona Turisme** (www.barcelonaturisme.com) provides details of accessible hotels and runs several accessible tours for wheelchair users and visitors with reduced mobility.

o Local tour companies are also making efforts to offer more accessible routes, such as **Barcelona Architecture Walks** (https://barcelonarchitecturewalks.com), which has some wheelchair-adapted itineraries.

o Several taxi companies have adapted vehicles, including **Greentaxi** (www.greentaxi.es).

o All Barcelona beaches now have accessible facilities, including adapted bathrooms and showers, wooden access ramps almost to the water and both visual and tactile signage. From April to September, volunteers at several beaches provide amphibious chairs and other assistance; some services require prior booking. Read more: www.barcelona.cat.

o Download Lonely Planet's free Accessible Travel guide from https://shop.lonelyplanet.com/categories/accessible-travel.com.

Business Hours

Banks 8.30am–2pm Monday to Friday; some also 4pm–7pm Thursday or 9am–1pm Saturday

Bars 6pm–2am (to 3am weekends)

Clubs Midnight–6am Thursday to Saturday

Museums & art galleries Vary considerably; generally 10am–8pm (though some shut for lunch around 2pm–4pm). Many close all day Monday and from 2pm Sunday.

Restaurants 1pm–4pm and 8.30pm–midnight; some open all day

Shops 9am or 10am–1.30pm or 2pm, and 4pm or 4.30pm–8pm or 8.30pm Monday to Saturday

Discount Cards

Arqueoticket (www.barcelonaturisme.com) Admission to four major

Warning: Watch Your Belongings

o Petty crime (bag-snatching, pickpocketing) is a major problem, especially in the city centre.

o You're especially vulnerable when dragging luggage to/from hotels; know your route.

o Avoid walking around El Raval and the southern end of La Rambla late at night.

o Take nothing of value to the beach and don't leave anything unattended.

history and archaeology galleries for €14.50.

Articket BCN (www.articketbcn.org) Admission to six major art galleries for €35.

Barcelona Card (www.barcelonacard.com) Costs €22/48/58/63 for two/three/four/five days; free transport and discounted or free sights admission.

Ruta del Modernisme (www.rutadelmodernisme.com) Modernista sights at discounted rates; costs €12.

Electricity

Type C
230V/50Hz

Media

Major Barcelona newspapers *La Vanguardia* (www.lavanguardia.com) and *El Periódico* (www.elperiodico.com) are available in Spanish and Catalan. *El País* (www.elpais.com) publishes in Spanish, Catalan and English.

Emergencies

All emergencies (ambulance, fire brigade etc)	112
EU standard emergency number	112
Country code	34
International access code	00

Money

o Credit and debit cards are accepted in most hotels, shops, restaurants and taxis. Since the COVID-19 pandemic, many places don't accept cash.

o ATMs are everywhere in central Barcelona.

Public Holidays

New Year's Day (Any Nou/Año Nuevo) 1 January

Epiphany/Three Kings' Day (Epifanía or El Dia dels Reis/Día de los Reyes Magos) 6 January

Good Friday (Divendres Sant/Viernes Santo) March/April

Easter Monday (Dilluns de Pasqua Florida/Lunes de Pascua) March/April

Labour Day (Dia del Treball/Fiesta del Trabajo) 1 May

Day after Pentecost Sunday (Dilluns de Pasqua Granada) May/June

Feast of St John the Baptist (Dia de Sant Joan/Día de San Juan Bautista) 24 June

Feast of the Assumption (L'Assumpció/La Asunción) 15 August

Catalonia's National Day (Diada Nacional de Catalunya) 11 September

Festes de la Mercè 24 September

Spanish National Day (Festa Nacional d'Espanya/Fiesta Nacional de España) 12 October

All Saints Day (Dia de Tots Sants/Día de

Todos los Santos)
1 November

Constitution Day (Dia de la Constitució/Día de la Constitución) 6 December

Feast of the Immaculate Conception (La Immaculada Concepció/La Inmaculada Concepción) 8 December

Christmas (Nadal/ Navidad) 25 December

Boxing Day/St Stephen's Day (Dia de Sant Esteve) 26 December

Telephone

∘ Travellers with phones from within the EU have free roaming.

∘ For others, an e-sim with a data package is a good option if your phone supports it. Otherwise, local SIM cards (available in Spanish phone shops) can be used in most unlocked phones.

Tipping

∘ **Bars** It's rare to tip in bars, though small change is appreciated.

∘ **Restaurants** Catalans typically leave 5% or less at restaurants. Leave more for good service.

∘ **Taxis** Optional, but most locals round up to the nearest euro.

Dos & Don'ts

∘ **Eating and drinking** In more casual restaurants, keep your cutlery between courses.

∘ **Escalators** Stand on the right to let people pass, especially on the metro.

∘ **Greetings** Catalans, like other Spaniards, usually greet friends and strangers alike with a kiss on both cheeks.

∘ **Visiting churches** It is considered disrespectful to visit churches as a tourist during Mass and other worship services. Taking photos at such times is a definite no-no, as is visiting without dressing appropriately.

Tourist Information

Aeroport del Prat (www.barcelonaturisme. com)

Catedral (Map p46, C2; www.barcelonaturisme. com)

Oficina de Turisme de Catalunya (Regional Tourist Office; https:// escasateva.catalunya.com)

Plaça de Catalunya (Map p62, C1; www. barcelonaturisme.com)

Visas

∘ **Citizens or residents of EU & Schengen countries** No visa required.

∘ **Citizens or residents of UK, Australia, Canada, Israel, Japan, New Zealand, the USA and most Latin American countries** From late 2023, nationals of these countries will require prior authorisation to enter Spain under the new European Travel Information and Authorisation System (ETIAS; www. etiasvisa.com). With ETIAS pre-authorisation, travellers can stay in Spain visa-free for 90 days within any given 180-day period.

∘ **Other countries** Check with a Spanish embassy or consulate.

Language

Both Spanish (known as *castellano*, or Castilian) and Catalan (*català*, spoken in Catalonia) are official languages in Spain. Eivissenc is the native dialect of Catalan spoken on Ibiza and Formentera. You'll be perfectly well understood speaking Spanish in Barcelona and you'll find that most locals will happily speak Spanish to you, especially once they realise you're a foreigner. Here we've provided you with some Spanish to get you started, as well as some Catalan basics at the end.

Just read our pronunciation guides as if they were English and you'll be understood. Note that (m/f) indicates masculine and feminine forms.

To enhance your trip with a phrasebook, visit **lonelyplanet.com**.

Basics

Hello.
Hola. · o·la

Goodbye.
Adiós. · a·dyos

How are you?
¿Qué tal? · ke tal

Fine, thanks.
Bien, gracias. · byen gra·thyas

Please.
Por favor. · por fa·vor

Thank you.
Gracias. · gra·thyas

Excuse me.
Perdón. · per·don

Sorry.
Lo siento. · lo syen·to

Yes./No.
Sí./No. · see/no

Do you speak (English)?
¿Habla (inglés)? · a·bla (een·gles)

I (don't) understand.
Yo (no) entiendo. · yo (no) en·tyen·do

Eating & Drinking

I'm a vegetarian. (m/f)
Soy · soy
vegetariano/a. · ve·khe·ta·rya·no/a

Cheers!
¡Salud! · sa·loo

That was delicious!
¡Estaba · es·ta·ba
buenísimo! · bwe·nee·see·mo

Please bring the bill.
Por favor nos · por fa·vor nos
trae la cuenta. · tra·e la kwen·ta

I'd like ...
Quisiera ... · kee·sye·ra ...

a coffee *un café* · oon ka·fe
a table *una mesa* · oo·na me·sa
for two *para dos* · pa·ra dos
a wine *un vino* · oon vee·no
two beers *dos* · dos
cervezas · ther·ve·thas

Shopping

I'd like to buy ...
Quisiera · kee·sye·ra
comprar ... · kom·prar ...

May I look at it?
¿Puedo verlo? · pwe·do ver·lo

How much is it?
¿Cuánto cuesta? · kwan·to kwes·ta

That's too/very expensive.
Es muy caro. · es mooy ka·ro

Emergencies

Help!
¡Socorro!   so·ko·ro

Call a doctor!
¡Llame a   *lya*·me a oon
un médico!   me·dee·ko

Call the police!
¡Llame a   *lya*·me a
la policía!   la po·lee·*thee*·a

I'm lost. (m/f)
Estoy perdido/a.   es·*toy* per·*dee*·do/a

I'm ill. (m/f)
Estoy enfermo/a.   es·*toy* en·*fer*·mo/a

Where are the toilets?
¿Dónde están   *don*·de es·*tan*
los baños?   los *ba*·nyos

Time & Numbers

What time is it?
¿Qué hora es?   ke o·ra es

It's (10) o'clock.
Son (las diez).   son (las dyeth)

morning	*mañana*	ma·*nya*·na
afternoon	*tarde*	*tar*·de
evening	*noche*	*no*·che
yesterday	*ayer*	a·*yer*
today	*hoy*	oy
tomorrow	*mañana*	ma·*nya*·na

1	*uno*	*oo*·no
2	*dos*	dos
3	*tres*	tres
4	*cuatro*	*kwa*·tro
5	*cinco*	*theen*·ko
6	*seis*	seys
7	*siete*	*sye*·te
8	*ocho*	*o*·cho
9	*nueve*	*nwe*·ve
10	*diez*	dyeth

Transport & Directions

Where's ...?
¿Dónde está ...?   *don*·de es·*ta* ...

What's the address?
¿Cuál es la   kwal es la
dirección?   dee·rek·*thyon*

Can you show me (on the map)?
¿Me lo puede   me lo *pwe*·de
indicar   een·dee·*kar*
(en el mapa)?   (en el *ma*·pa)

I want to go to ...
Quisiera ir a ...   kee·*sye*·ra eer a ...

What time does it arrive/leave?
¿A qué hora   a ke o·ra
llega/sale?   *lye*·ga/sa·le

I want to get off here.
Quiero bajarme   *kye*·ro ba·*khar*·me
aquí.   a·*kee*

Catalan – Basics

Good morning.
Bon dia.   bon *dee*·a

Good afternoon.
Bona tarda.   bo·na *tar*·da

Good evening.
Bon vespre.   bon *bes*·pra

Goodbye.
Adéu.   a·*the*·oo

Please.
Sisplau.   sees·*pla*·oo

Thank you.
Gràcies.   *gra*·see·a

You're welcome.
De res.   de res

Excuse me.
Perdoni.   par·*tho*·nee

I'm sorry.
Ho sento.   oo *sen*·to

How are you?
Com estàs?   kom as·*tas*

Very well.
(Molt) Bé.   (mol) be

Behind the Scenes

Send Us Your Feedback

We love to hear from travellers – your comments help make our books better. We read every word, and we guarantee that your feedback goes straight to the authors. Visit **lonelyplanet.com/contact** to submit your updates and suggestions.

Note: We may edit, reproduce and incorporate your comments in Lonely Planet products such as guidebooks, websites and digital products, so let us know if you are happy to have your name acknowledged. For a copy of our privacy policy visit **lonelyplanet.com/legal**.

Isabella's Thanks

An enormous *gràcies* to everyone who helped out on all things Barcelona: Sally Davies, Esme Fox, Marwa El-Hennawey Preston, Tom Stainer, the Devour team, Clementina Milà, Joan Pau Aragón, María del Río, Vera de Frutos, Suzy Taher, Isabelle Kliger, Nigel Haywood, Alex Pérez, Lorna Turnbull, José Fabra and friends, Pau Gavaldà, David Doyes, and Ariadna and family. As always, the biggest thanks (and salut!) to my loyal research assistants Jack Noble, John Noble and Andrew Brannan.

Acknowledgements

Cover photographs: Night view of Magic Fountain light show, Boule/Shutterstock ©; Tapas bar, Jayme Wiseman/Shutterstock © Photographs pp 34–5 (clockwise from top left): Kauka Jarvi/Shutterstock ©; Mario Marco/Getty Images ©; Gimas/Shutterstock © architect: Richard Meier; Catarina Belova/Shutterstock ©

Behind the Scenes

This Book

This 8th edition of Lonely Planet's *Pocket Barcelona* guidebook was researched and written by Isabella Noble. The previous edition was also written by Isabella and the 6th edition was written by Sally Davies and Catherine Le Nevez.

This guidebook was produced by the following:

Commissioning Editor Kate Chapman

Production Editor Sofie Andersen

Cartographer Julie Sheridan

Book Designers Katherine Marsh, Mazzy Prinsep

Assisting Editors Shauna Daly, Simon Williamson

Cover Researcher Fergal Condon

Thanks to Ronan Abayawickrema, Melanie Dankel, Bruce Evans, Karen Henderson, Ania Lenihan, Amy Lysen, Vivek Shinde

Index

See also separate subindexes for:

⊗ **Eating p190**

◉ **Drinking p191**

✪ **Entertainment p191**

🔒 **Shopping p191**

Our Writer

Isabella Noble

@isabellamnoble
British-Australian on paper and brought up in Málaga, bilingual travel journalist Isabella has been exploring Spain for decades, and currently splits her time between Barcelona, Andalucía and Toronto. She is a Spain specialist for Lonely Planet, the *Telegraph*, the *Guardian*, Condé Nast Traveller, Ink, GeoPlaneta, British Airways High Life and more, as well as an editor, translator, hotel reviewer and Spanish-language writer. She also writes about India, Thailand, Greece, the UK, Australia and beyond. Read more at isabellanoble.com.

Writer's Thanks

Moltes gràcies to everyone who helped out on this project, particularly the local experts who contributed their own Barcelona tips. Thanks to Inés Miró-Sans, Carme Ruscalleda, Pia Wortham, Stef Roth, Isabelle Kliger, Aida Falip, Miguel Ángel Borràs, Montse Ruiz, Suzanne Wales, Pau Gavaldá, Montse Salvadó, Sally Davies, Esme Fox, Jamie Ditaranto, Arantxa Domínguez, Joel Miñana and many others, and to top research assistants John Noble and Joanna Lally, as well as Jack Noble, Andrew Brannan and Daniel Westwood for all the support.

Published by Lonely Planet Global Limited
CRN 554153
8th edition
ISBN 978 1 83869 176 9
© Lonely Planet 2023 Photographs © as indicated 2023
10 9 8 7 6 5 4 3 2
Printed in Malaysia